D1643866

Ashford
from Steam to Eurostar

Compiled by
Vic
Mitchell

MP Middleton Press

Cover pictures:
Upper - Passengers from Paris speed through Ashford in the
"Golden Arrow" Pullman cars behind the Southern Railway's
"King Arthur" class 4-6-0 no. E863 Lord Rodney *and their*
luggage vans in 1930. (Pamlin Prints)
Lower - Racing along the same up fast line on 11th October 1995,
passengers from Paris would reach London in less than half the
time by Eurostar. Finishing work was being undertaken on
Britain's first international through platforms on the left.
(V.Mitchell)

**This book is published to commemorate Ashford's
attainment of a place on the international
railway map on 8th January 1996.**

First published January 1996

ISBN 1 873793 67 7

© *Middleton Press 1996*

Design - Deborah Goodridge

Typesetting - Barbara Mitchell

Published by Middleton Press
        Easebourne Lane
        Midhurst
        West Sussex
        GU29 9AZ
        Tel: 01730 813169
        Fax: 01730 812601

Printed & bound by Biddles Ltd,
        Guildford and Kings Lynn

CONTENTS

ACKNOWLEDGEMENTS

Grateful thanks are expressed to all those who have contributed chapters to this volume. They have also provided the photographs therein unless credited to other photographers. Thanks also go to those cameramen who have exercised their skills for our pleasure. Appreciation is also due for the assistance received from J.Creed, D.Cullum, L.Harvey, B.Haste, A.Ll. Lambert, N.Langridge, Mr.D & Dr.S.Salter and A.Saunders.

INTRODUCTION

Having been involved in the production of five railway route albums featuring Ashford (listed on the last page of this book), I felt frustrated that there had been no opportunity to present this important railway centre in a coordinated logical manner, although each set of photographs are in chronological order.

Gordon Turner gives immense details of the early decades of the railways of Ashford in his *Ashford - the coming of the railway*, whilst Adrian Gray in his *London Chatham & Dover Railway* and his *South Eastern Railway* sets Ashford in the complex developing railway scene.

Local railway heritage activist Roger Airey wrote to me suggesting that the opening of Ashford International should not pass without a commemorative booklet. I proposed that the title should take the form of a station announcement - "ASHFORD ... THIS IS ASHFORD ..." with the subtitle "CHANGE HERE FOR EUROPE". On reflection, it dawned on me that this was the time to bring together, in book form, a number of earlier essays and combine them with contributions from present day specialists to create the sought after coordinated record.

As publisher, I set the book size to our normal 96 pages only to find myself disappointed, as the compiler, having to condense some sections and omit others. Whilst I would like to have written "Ashford's Railway Stations and Works" (probably requiring several volumes), we must satisfy ourselves with a selection of aspects of Ashford's railway past and present. I hope that they will be enjoyed on their own and enhanced by the material contained in our other publications.

Vic Mitchell

Midhurst
November 1995

1. HISTORICAL BACKGROUND
Vic Mitchell

he South Eastern Railway started the first train service between London and Ashford on 1st December 1842. The route was via Redhill, a more direct line having been ruled out by Parliament. It was thought that only one railway south of London was desirable, politicians (then, as now) thinking they knew how best to run railways. Travellers had to wait until 1868 for the more direct route via Sevenoaks.

Ashford ceased to be a terminus on 28th June 1843, when the line was extended to Folkestone. Ashford's first station was a simple board clad structure, probably similar to that still standing at nearby Pluckley in 1995.

Pre 1899 ownership of the main lines
of Kent. (Railway Magazine)

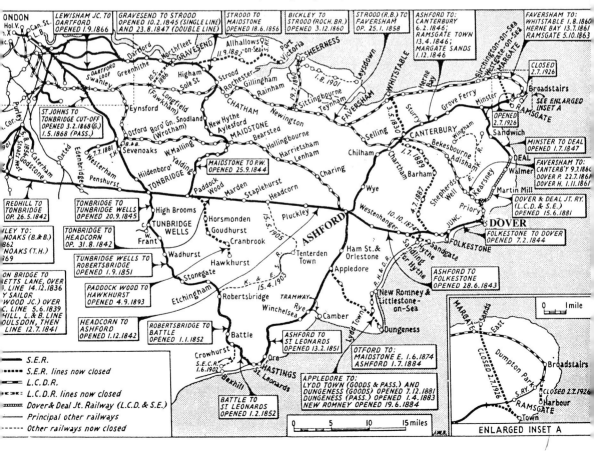

The far sighted SER provided two through lines between the two platform loop lines at Ashford and at several other stations on its main line. Each platform had its own carriage shed and coke shed (locomotives did not burn coal at that time). South of the station there were docks for horses, horse-drawn carriages and cattle. To the north there were coal wharves and a goods shed.

Ashford became a junction on 6th February 1846 when the branch to Canterbury opened, followed by a line to Hastings on 13th February 1851, bay platforms having been provided for these services.

The SER monopoly in Kent was gradually eroded by the London, Chatham & Dover Railway. It extended its Swanley - Maidstone line to Ashford and commenced services on 1st July 1884. The terminus was situated west of the town; a link with the SER had to wait until 1892.

After decades of ruinous and expensive competition, the two rivals agreed to operation by a joint managing committee from 1st January 1899, using the title South Eastern & Chatham Railway. Immediately Ashford West station was closed to passengers, all Maidstone line trains running into the former SER station. The terminal site remained in use for goods traffic.

The SECR became part of the Southern Railway in 1923, which in turn was nationalised in 1948 to become a constituent of British Railways. Ashford was within the Southern Region, which became part of Network SouthEast in 1986. More recently, most services have been operated under the name of "South East Trains", as a prelude to proposed privatisation.

Established in 1847, Ashford Works is detailed in the next nine chapters. Although the SR discontinued steam locomotive construction therein in 1936, repair work was undertaken there until 1962. Further batches of locomotives were built during and after World War II. Wagon construction kept much of the Works busy until 1981. Thereafter only small areas of the premises were used for railway purposes.

Major changes took place in 1961 with the advent of electrification and the establishment of the associated Chart Leacon Repair Shop west of the station. The mid-1990s heralded even greater alterations with the creation of the International Passenger Station.

Plans for the biggest railway project yet were announced; this being the construction of a new high speed line by Union Railways between Ashford and London.

The 1871 edition Ordnance Survey map at 6ins to 1 mile has London - Folkestone line from top to bottom; the branch to Canterbury is on the right and the Hastings line is on the left. The LCDR terminus was opened later, near the cattle market. New Town was built by the SER to house its workers, all the dwellings facing onto a triangular green. Note the fields and orchards between the station and the town centre.

2. ESTABLISHMENT OF ASHFORD WORKS
Southern Railway 1947 booklet

 T was in the February of the year 1846 that the Board of Directors of the South Eastern Railway decided to buy, for the sum of £21,000, from a gentleman of the name of Walls, 185 acres of good Kentish countryside (which included a farm house, or two) on which to lay the foundations of—to quote the term in use at the time—a " Locomotive Establishment."

This seed-ground of early Victorian enterprise lay at Ashford ; a little beyond the station, on the Folkestone side—excellently situated in regard to several of the more important stations on the railway, such as Redhill, Tonbridge, Tunbridge Wells, Maidstone, Canterbury, Folkestone and Dover.

Parliamentary endorsement to a proposal to expend up to £500,000 on this new venture had been sought and secured, and in March we find the Directors reporting to the proprietors (not without a shade of complacency) that they had " purchased the land requisite for these purposes, on advantageous terms, and in the situation where they wished to have it."

Shortly after the Board's decision to build the Works—less than four months, in fact—we find the Archbishop of Canterbury expressing grave concern over the inadequacy of the existing church accommodation at Ashford, in view of the large number of men it was alleged would be employed there. A grant of £100 is thereupon offered by the Directors towards the stipend of a " pastoral super-intendent," to be appointed specially for the purpose of ministering to the spiritual needs of these men and, in course of time, the Rev. John Pughe comes to Ashford to fulfil this requirement.

Then, in the summer of 1847, in the humble shape of a cluster of seventy-two labourers' cottages, there arose the first unpretentious signs that yet another new railway project—in that era of railway development—had been launched. The story of Ashford Works had begun.

So rapid was the progress at this stage that we find, by September, a room in a block of these same cottages being utilised for an inaugural meeting of the " Ashford Works Mechanics' Institute." Here, after telling this pioneer gathering of young artisans how impossible it was to foresee the full extent to which any new enterprise in those fruitful days might not develop, the Chairman of the Board (Mr. J. MacGregor) gave details of the plans, which had been drawn up over a twelvemonth previously, for the construction not merely of a fine and well-equipped locomotive works at Ashford, but of a complete village also, in which the men employed there might make

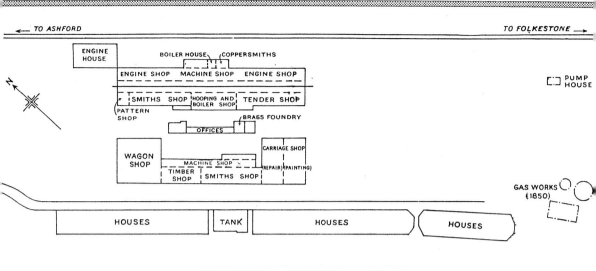

ENGINE HOUSE

BOILER HOUSE   COPPERSMITHS

ENGINE SHOP   MACHINE SHOP   ENGINE SHOP

PUMP HOUSE

SMITHS SHOP   HOOPING AND BOILER SHOP   TENDER SHOP

PATTERN SHOP

BRASS FOUNDRY

OFFICES

WAGON SHOP

CARRIAGE SHOP

MACHINE SHOP

(REPAIR)(PAINTING)

TIMBER SHOP   SMITHS SHOP

HOUSES

TANK

HOUSES

HOUSES

GAS WORKS (1850)

ASHFORD   WORKS — 1847

their homes.   There, too, would be built a school for their children,
a house of worship, public baths and washing premises, and a building
for the newly born Institute whose natal day they were that moment
celebrating.   The Directors were thereupon enrolled as members of
the Institute and gave each a book to its library.   And in his speech
of welcome one of the audience sketched the wonderful transformation
scene unfolding before all their eyes and reflected on how quickly a
great Works and a new village were springing up in a place where
there had been " not long since fields seldom trodden, except by the
foot of the herdsman."

In imaginative conception, the "railway village," as it was later to
become—possessing its own general shop, its own public baths, its
airy, spacious green on the doorsteps of the workpeople's homes, even
its own "pub" (the "Alfred Arms")—was surely an astonishing piece
of anticipation. For what in principle have our ultra-progressive town-
planning programmes of to-day to offer, that this South Eastern Railway scheme did not provide the Ashford Works employees nearly
one hundred years ago ?

At the autumn half-yearly meeting of the South Eastern company
in 1847 the Directors were able to give the news officially that the
transference of the Railway's locomotive depot from New Cross
(where the company had secured temporarily the sole rights to the
use of certain locomotive buildings there belonging to the Brighton
and Croydon companies) to the new site at Ashford was proceeding
towards completion.

From the start of the year, however, a limited amount of locomotive repair and maintenance work had been taking place at

Ashford; the engines, without exception, being those ordered from outside contractors. Now, in 1848, work began on the first locomotive actually to be completed at the new Works. This was a little engine, remarkable alike for its vertical boiler and small dimensions, nicknamed "The Coffee Pot," and designed for the purpose of propelling the Company's Directors and chief engineer about the South Eastern system on their periodical inspections of the line. Officially designated "No. 126," it possessed outside cylinders $5\frac{3}{4}$ ins. diameter by 9 ins. stroke, 3 ft. 6 ins. diameter wheels and a boiler barrel of diameter 2 ft. 6 ins. The tank capacity was 130 gallons and the driver was accommodated in a recess immediately over the axle of the carrying wheels. Having been partially constructed at Brick-

This Nasmythe, Gaskell belt driven wall drill was in use for over a century.

An eastward view from the 1860s includes the Clock Tower on the right and contemporary coaches.

layers' Arms, "The Coffee Pot" remained a stock job at Ashford until its completion in 1850 ; and its active railway service lasted until 1861, when it was taken off the line and sent to do pump-house duty at Redhill. Its design is attributed to a marine engineer of the name of Fernihough.

Nicknamed "The Coffee Pot", this unusual engine was completed in Ashford Works in 1850.

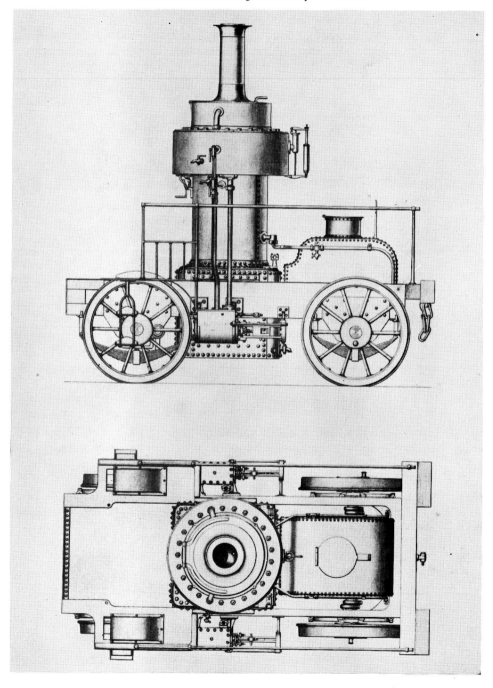

The autumn of 1850 saw the creation of the Carriage and Wagon department at Ashford. By this time the adjoining railway village, known at first by the name of " Alfred Town," but later referred to as " Ashford New Town," had been extended by another sixty houses and, furthermore, the utilitarian outlines of a gas-works were making their appearance on the site. It has been recorded that the rent charged their employees by the South Eastern company was 3s. 6d., but that the tenants had to pay their own gas bills.

By the end of the following year the Works were supporting nearly 3,000 people—including, that is, the workpeople's wives and families —and the wheels were really beginning to hum within the long buildings. Then, in 1853, Ashford Works was turning out its first standard design locomotives.

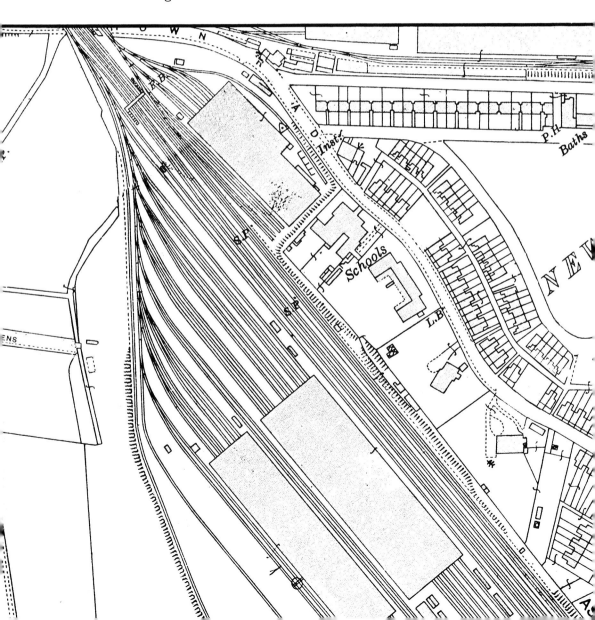

New Town was created by the SER to provide accommodation and all necessities close to the Works. A triangular "village green" surrounded by trees was an unusual feature of contemporary industrial housing schemes.

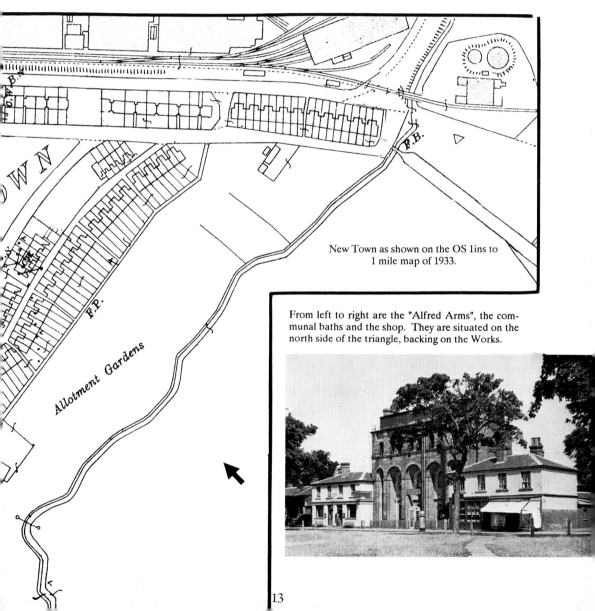

New Town as shown on the OS 1ins to 1 mile map of 1933.

From left to right are the "Alfred Arms", the communal baths and the shop. They are situated on the north side of the triangle, backing on the Works.

3. THE CUDWORTH ERA 1853
Southern Railway 1947 booklet

OR several years past the destinies of the locomotive department of the South Eastern Railway had been in the hands of that engineer of ability, James I'Anson Cudworth, who had also been responsible for the selection of much of the equipment for the new Works. At Ashford, now, he began to produce his first locomotives for the South Eastern. These were long-boilered 2–4–0 passenger engines, with outside frames and a compensating beam above the bearings, earmarked for a creditable reputation under the title of the " Hastings " or No. 157 class. Cudworth was a locomotive designer who believed in making experiments—it was he who had been the first to apply the " uniflow " system of steam distribution to a railway engine—and he now gave trial to yet another novel idea, a firebox divided by a longitudinal water partition, or " midfeather," and possessing sloping grates, the aim of these being to make it possible for coal fuel to be used without causing the emission of smoke. Hitherto, the staple diet of a railway engine's firebox had been coke, in regard to which problems of smoke abatement had not arisen. Eventually, all the engines in Cudworth's charge were equipped with his firebox, and the device remained standard in the design of South Eastern locomotives for over thirty years—that is, fifteen years after Cudworth had resigned from the company. Another idea that Cudworth tested was the placing of the sandbox on the top of the boiler barrel (under the dome) ; successful in that the heat of the boiler was utilised effectively to keep the sand dry, but unpractical in that spilt sand at the time of refilling was calculated to fall just where it was least useful—in the mechanism—and discontinued in the end for that reason.

After building a number of goods and passenger engines of various classes to Cudworth's designs, Ashford now (1861) produced a masterpiece, by the same author, in the elegant shape of the first of his " Mail " class locomotives. These fine 7-ft. " Singles," created specifically for hauling the fast London to Dover " Post Office " expresses, were the mainstay of the main line working on the South Eastern Railway for twenty-five years. Rous-Marten noted in 1884 how No. 204 hauled the Dover express, of 150 tons, from Cannon Street to passing Ashford, 54¾ miles, in 74 minutes. Known among their admirers of those days affectionately as the " Flyers," or the " Free-wheelers," it was said of them that (for a short run involving only one stoppage for water) they were the fastest in England..

No. 130 was built in the Works to Cudworth's design in 1863. The child's clothes suggest that the photograph might be from that date.

It is interesting to find, in George Measom's *Official Guide to the South Eastern Railway*, a description of Ashford Works as he found the depot at about the time that these engines were being built within its shops :

" These [the locomotive and carriage shops] consist of the large engine shed, 280 feet long, by sixty-four feet wide. The total length of the workshop is 396 feet. The engine-repairing shop is 254 feet long, by forty-five feet wide ; the large crane, capable of lifting twenty tons, traverses over this part. The machine shop, or turnery, is 142 feet long, by 45 feet wide. Over the engine-house which adjoins this part of the building is a tank, holding 54,700 gallons of water. The tender shop is seventy-two feet long, by forty-five feet wide. The smith's shop is 174 feet long, by forty-five feet wide and contains twenty fires. The wheel-hooping and boiler shop is 142 feet long, by sixty feet wide. . . . The length of the carriage and truck house is 645 feet, capable of holding fifty carriages and eighty trucks. The store-room is 216 feet long, by forty feet wide, and is a perfect model of neatness. Here is deposited every article which can by possibility be required, from things the most unwieldy and huge in bulk to the most diminutive screws, and the whole arranged with the greatest precision and even elegance."

Built in 1865, this is one of the Cudworth's famous "Mail" engines with 7ft driving wheels. The chimney was a later modification. The sand box is beside the dome.

Incidentally, Cudworth had installed at Ashford the entire working motion of one of his goods engines (No. 106)—this for the purpose of giving practical demonstrations in the action of valves, and so forth, to men undergoing training for footplate duties.

An event taking place outside the boundaries of Ashford Works at about this time, yet fairly claiming the right to be included in its story, was the dedication and opening of Christ Church, in South Ashford. The cost of building this church (not to be formally consecrated until Bishop Marsden's visit in 1889) was met almost entirely by sums subscribed voluntarily by the shareholders of the South Eastern Railway Company. Further, up to 1937 the Southern company made an annual grant of £100 towards the maintenance and upkeep of this unique "railway" church.

In 1876, as the outcome of the provoking behaviour of high authority in commissioning Ramsbottom of the London and North Western to design a class of passenger engine for the South Eastern over his unwitting head, Cudworth resigned, and his chair at Ashford was, somewhat over-hastily, filled by A. M. Watkin, the son of the Chairman, Sir Edward Watkin. But the former's labours in the good cause of the South Eastern locomotive establishment were, alas, to be commemorated solely in the name " Watkin's express engines," commonly bestowed on the twenty Ramsbottom locomotives, in the designing of which the new chief at Ashford had taken no hand.

Watkin's successor, R. C. Mansell, who had been Carriage and Wagon superintendent during this time, had already brought distinction to the South Eastern by his creation of the " Mansell " wheel for carriage stock. This—yet another successful Ashford innovation—was steel-tyred and composed of teak segments, weighed in pairs and chosen for their perfect symmetry. They were forced on to the axles by an hydraulic pressure equal to 60 tons, no key whatsoever being used to secure them in position. Entirely satisfactory as had been the " Mansell " wheels for coaching stock—and certain unkind critics had been known to observe that they were the only praiseworthy features of the South Eastern carriages at that period— an attempt to apply the principle to a locomotive's wheels (a goods engine, No. 127, was the guinea pig) met with seemingly insoluble problems associated with loosened tyres.

Three classes of engines were built during Mansell's interim term of office—and then there made its appearance among the machines and benches at Ashford the striking figure (with its integral commanding personality) of James Stirling, straight from the north, firm disciplinarian and railway pioneer.

This all second class coach has oil lighting and Mansell's wood-centred wheels.

4. THE STIRLING ERA 1878
Southern Railway 1947 booklet

TIRLING, soon to become greatly esteemed among the staff of the Works, quickly had his first class of passenger engines, 4–4–0 s with 6-ft. driving wheels, running over the lines of the South Eastern. He was a designer who saw no need for the steam dome in locomotive design and consequently all the engines that came out of Ashford in his time were without this traditional feature. He was, likewise, a man who saw no necessity for the outer world to be notified of what was going forward within the confines of his Works, and paid his small son pocket-money to scan through all the technical journals for news items naming Ashford, in order that he might call down fire and slaughter on the heads of the offending editors. He painted his engines (up to 1895) black, with red lines, equipping them all with his own labour-saving steam reversing device, which might not have become an adjunct of loco-motive design for some years had not his mother once expressed to him the compassion she felt towards certain perspiring enginemen she had seen hauling over the heavy reversing gear of their locomotive by muscular strength alone.

After building various standard goods engines, and a class of 0–4–4 tanks, to Stirling's designs, Ashford proceeded to produce the initial model of his handsome and successful "F" class bogie expresses,

Stirling's F class 4-4-0 no. 240 **Onward** won a Gold Medal at the Paris Exhibition of 1889.

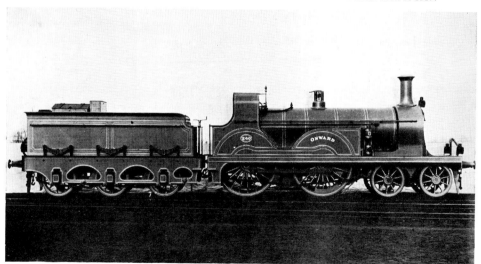

with 7-ft. driving wheels, No. 240 of which won for its creator a Gold Medal award at the 1889 Paris Exhibition. The engines selected for entry at these competitions, held at eleven-yearly intervals in Paris—the last taking place in 1900—were shipped across the Channel from Newhaven to Dieppe. One may see at Newhaven to this day sheerlegs that were erected specially for the purpose of loading the exhibition locomotives on to the steamers.

Of the passenger stock in service in Stirling's time, this extract from Foxwell's *Express Trains*, of 1888, gives a traveller's impression :

> " The third class carriages on the Ramsgate and Hastings trains are more roomy than the average in England. The passengers' communication with the guard is far superior to that mockery provided on our great lines of the North."

This comment is interesting in view of the fact that, in an endeavour to swell the revenue of the company, Sir Edward Watkin, the Chairman, was then strongly in favour of *not* increasing the comforts available to third class passengers—in order to drive them, in sheer desperation, into first and second class compartments. The national character being the tough thing that it is, however, third class travelling thrived.

Before the effects of his salient personality withdrew from Ashford (he resigned at the formation of the South Eastern and Chatham Joint Committee in 1899), James Stirling was elected a member of the Institution of Mechanical Engineers and later received the honour of the Presidential chair at the Association of Locomotive Engineers.

And, incidentally, it is to his inflexible aversion for photographers and their productions that we owe a dearth of photographs both of Stirling and of the fine engines that he created.

SER Boat Train coach of 1891 outside the Works.

5. THE WAINWRIGHT ERA 1899
Southern Railway 1947 booklet

FTER Stirling—the Wainwright era at Ashford ; this time, however, *not* to be introduced with the appearance of an unfamiliar figure in the shops. For three years previously, Harry S. Wainwright had been in charge of the carriage and wagon section at the Works. It had been his triumph to have designed for the South Eastern the famous " Folkestone Car Train " of vestibuled coaches, which was at one time the only complete train of its kind in the United Kingdom. Although this train had not actually been constructed at Ashford, it was a very handsome indication of a new and progressive policy in regard to carriage building that was now to become manifest at the Works. The carriage and wagon department was now divided into two parts : the one known as the " cradle " and the other as the " hospital "—terms sufficiently illuminating to render interpretation unnecessary. It was the time when steel was just beginning to oust wood in the construction of underframes, although in the saw-mill were still to be seen huge quantities of pitch pine stacked, together with Quebec oak and a variety of finer woods. Here, also, was to be seen a complete automatic fire-extinguishing plant, with 1,200 sprinklers—and this was the only railway shop of its kind in England to be so equipped.

Lavish luxury was provided for wealthy passengers travelling between London and Folkestone.

Unbelievable comfort was given to first-class passengers in the "Folkestone Car Train".

Ashford could boast, too, several machines novel for those days, such as a "coke-crusher"—all coke crushing formerly having been done by hand—and an American-built mitring machine.

To "fix" the period, we quote this evocative description of the Lamp-making Shop, published in the '90's :

"Even should the electric light be adopted throughout the South Eastern system (and let it be here stated that every new coach is being so fitted, on Stone's well-known system), the occupation of the workmen employed in this building would be by no means gone. Everything, from the footwarmer to the mug for the annual school treat, is constructed in this shop."

The latest type of ordinary passenger coach under construction at that date was a 44-ft. composite bogie corridor, with lavatories in the centre and lounge seats at the ends. A step towards refining the æsthetic qualities of the interior of passenger vehicles was made in these carriages, where the ceilings of both the compartments and of the corridors were made semi-elliptical. It seems likely, too, that in these carriages the door leading into the corridor was first provided with its (now familiar) sliding window.

When guiding the affairs of the carriage and wagon department alone, Wainwright had brought about many improvements in the shops. One can assume that his ample moustaches bristled with

The traverser in the Erecting Shop was steam driven until the advent of electricity.

A continuous series of turntables provided a novel means of moving wheelsets in the Erecting Shop in 1901.

displeasure at the sight of such enemies of health and efficiency as low roofing, poor lighting and bad ventilation, for he saw that such defects were quickly remedied. And he devised many ingenious methods for reducing the discomforts inevitably associated with certain branches of the work.

In 1898, the year prior to his appointment to the superintendency of the whole Works, a new shop was built, on fresh ground, between the main establishment and the Hastings line. Whether or not the name " Klondyke " that was bestowed on this new building was intended for a verbal salute to the " get-rich-quick " spirit that may have prompted the enterprise, or whether (for much the same reason) it had been the name already given to some sidings previously in existence at this point it is difficult to say ; the fact remains that the building has been known by that romantic title to this very day.

Once the South Eastern and Chatham Working Agreement had been signed, in 1899, it became one of Wainwright's earliest jobs to paint the " Chatham" stock in the sovereign purple lake, lined finely in gold, of the South Eastern carriages, and to convert it to electric lighting and automatic vacuum brakes. In those colourful times the standard livery of the South Eastern engines was Brunswick green, decorated with broad bands of a lighter green and thin lines of yellow and red.

Soon after the turn of the century Ashford was giving employment to some 2,500 men and boys, and the buildings extended over an area of 53 acres, 12 of which were roofed over and the remainder used for storage and transportation purposes. A further 68 acres were held in readiness for future developments. The latest addition to the shops beyond the Hastings line had been named " Kimberley," possibly in imitation of the previous christening.

In the Mechanics' Institute classes for the Works' staff were regularly being held in such subjects as machine drawing and construction, railway carriage building, French, shorthand, arithmetic and geometry, and so many of the boys that had been educated in the South Eastern school were being accepted at the Works for training, that much competition arose among parents living in the district to have their sons admitted to the school.

During his years of office as Locomotive, Carriage and Wagon Superintendent, Wainwright produced some well-proportioned and resplendent engines. Highly polished brass dome coverings distinguished his creations, some classes being further embellished with copper-sheathed chimney tops. Between 1900 and 1908, seventy six-coupled goods engines to his design were built in the Works, and in the period 1901–1907 he also constructed twenty-one of his famous 4–4–0 "D" class express locomotives. Further, in 1905 appeared his class "E" expresses, and early in 1909 the first of a small class of 0–6–0 side-tank engines.

This was, in fact, an era of great productivity at Ashford. Soon after the amalgamation with the " Chatham " line, the works at

This was the scene in the Locomotive shop at Ashford Works about the period 1905-06.

Putting the finishing touches to South Eastern and Chatham stock in the Carriage Paint shop in the same period.

In these days every machine has its own electric motor. In 1906, all the machines were driven by belts worked from a main steam power unit.

The Boiler Shop as it appeared in 1906. In the centre of the picture is a pneumatic hoist.

The Locomotive Iron Foundry in 1905-06. The overhead traverser in the background was entirely hand-operated.

Where the lamps received overhaul. This corner of the Works altered considerably in the passing years.

Longhedge, Battersea, wherein many a reliable engine had been built for the London, Chatham and Dover company, passed over to Ashford the locomotive construction and (later) the repair work that had formerly been carried out in its sheds, and this added burden made it necessary for considerable extensions to be made to the Works.

In 1909 there were 497 engines on the South Eastern section, for the repair and maintenance of which Ashford Works was responsible. At that date the " Chatham and Dover " line possessed 257 loco-motives—so it will be seen why the closing of the latter company's depot called for an increase of practically fifty per cent. in the working capacity of Ashford. This was a situation demanding a large-scale expansion of the Works. Consequently, in 1909 a plan of the necessary extensions to be made was drawn up and a year or two later the work itself was completed.

Thus we find that the existing Boiler shop was extended to the east —absorbing pits previously used for engine repairs—and that an entirely new Erecting shop was constructed, 580 feet long and capable of dealing with 28 locomotives. In addition, the old Erecting shop received various extensions and to allow for the necessary enlarge-ment of both the Machine shop and the Fitting shop, a new Tender shop was built. The existing Pattern shop became the Smith shop (also enlarged) and the old Wagon Sheeting shop (as being conveniently adjacent to the Iron Foundry) was taken over by the Pattern Makers. Finally, the Paint shop was made bigger by fifty per cent.

Then in 1912 a milestone was passed when, with the opening of a Power House sheltering two D.C. generators, electricity made its presence felt, for the first time, at Ashford. This plant was reinforced later by a third generator and eventually a future day was to see the addition of a rectifier to enable A.C. current from the grid to be employed. With the arrival of electric power came the conversion of all the overhead cranes to electric drive.

In this year there commenced a very necessary enlargement of the "New Town." Work began on the construction of an additional 126 six-roomed dwellings, of improved design, bringing the total number of houses to 272. While this building activity was proceeding, to meet a pressing need a second railway school, up-to-date in design and equip-ment, for girls, was opened less than a hundred yards from the earlier one, which was now to be devoted exclusively to the education of boys and infants.

But the year also saw the administration of the long-established mechanics' classes pass from the hands of the railway company to the Kent Education Committee. No longer was the old S.E.R. Mechanics' Institute to be a centre for technical instruction. Instead, the premises (managed by a committee of railwaymen elected annually) were to be thrown open for social purposes, financed by subscriptions deducted from the members' pay packets, backed up by the liberal grant of £100 (later increased to £125) per annum from the company's

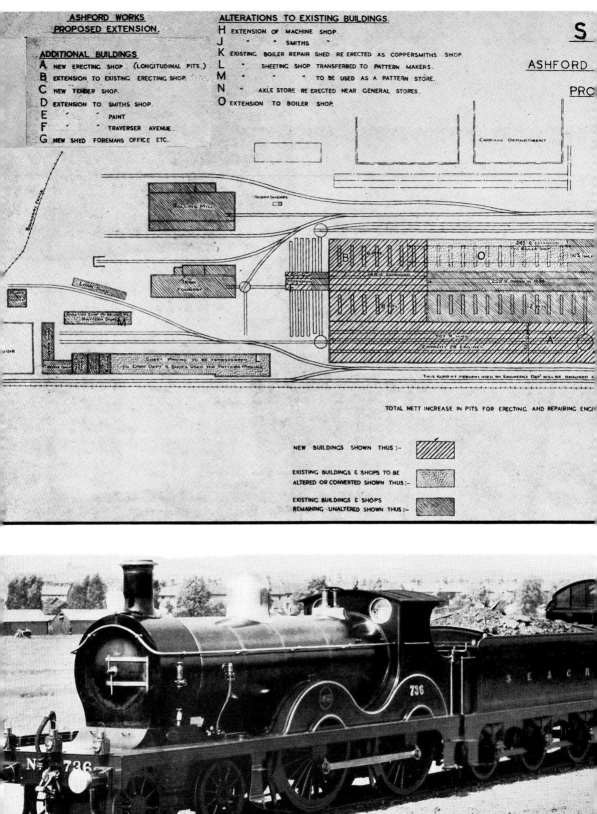

ASHFORD WORKS
PROPOSED EXTENSION.

ALTERATIONS TO EXISTING BUILDINGS.

H EXTENSION OF MACHINE SHOP.
J " " SMITHS "
K EXISTING BOILER REPAIR SHED RE ERECTED AS COPPERSMITHS SHOP.
L " SHEETING SHOP TRANSFERRED TO PATTERN MAKERS.
M " " " TO BE USED AS A PATTERN STORE.
N " AXLE STORE RE ERECTED NEAR GENERAL STORES.
O EXTENSION TO BOILER SHOP.

S
ASHFORD
PRO

ADDITIONAL BUILDINGS

A NEW ERECTING SHOP (LONGITUDINAL PITS.)
B EXTENSION TO EXISTING ERECTING SHOP.
C NEW TENDER SHOP.
D EXTENSION TO SMITHS SHOP.
E " " PAINT "
F " " TRAVERSER AVENUE.
G NEW SHED FOREMANS OFFICE ETC.

CARRIAGE DEPARTMENT

ROLLING MILL

SCRAP SHEARS

IRON FOUNDRY

LOCO SHED

PATTERN SHOP

M

SHEET MAKING TO BE TRANSFERRED
TO CARR DEPT & SHOPS USED FOR PATTERN MAKING

L

CAPACITY 28 ENGINES

THIS ROAD AT PRESENT USED BY ENGINEERS DEPT WILL BE REQUIRED F

TOTAL NETT INCREASE IN PITS FOR ERECTING AND REPAIRING ENGI

NEW BUILDINGS SHOWN THUS :—

EXISTING BUILDINGS & SHOPS TO BE
ALTERED OR CONVERTED SHOWN THUS :—

EXISTING BUILDINGS & SHOPS
REMAINING UNALTERED SHOWN THUS :—

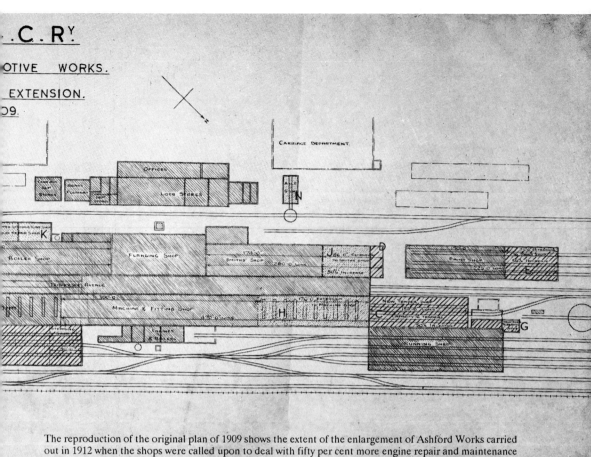

The reproduction of the original plan of 1909 shows the extent of the enlargement of Ashford Works carried out in 1912 when the shops were called upon to deal with fifty per cent more engine repair and maintenance work, following the closure of the former London, Chatham and Dover company's locomotive works at Longhedge, Battersea.

A handsome train of the 1900s. It is the South Eastern and Chatham company's London-Dover "Continental Express," headed by an Ashford-built Wainwright D class engine, no. 736.

exchequer. A variety of sports clubs, and an Engineering, Literary and Debating Society, were associated with this re-created Institute, and the Works' excellent voluntary Band—a source of pleasure at many a summer flower show or fête, and destined one day to become a memorable feature in a B.B.C. "In Town To-night" broadcast—came under its Council.

It was in the year following (1913) that the last Wainwright engines to be built at Ashford left the shops. These were five six-coupled trailing bogie tanks of a class entirely new, not only for the S.E.&C.R. but for any line situated south of the metropolis. Yet the Works had not, as it happened, seen the last of new designs by Wainwright. At the beginning of the fateful year 1914, after Wainwright himself had retired, the management placed an order with a Manchester firm for a number of large 4–4–0 engines, the plans for which had been laid down by Wainwright during the closing months of his administration. Estimating, however, that an additional ten would be urgently needed by the middle of the year, and being unable to find a British manufacturer prepared to deliver the engines in time, the company finally placed the order with the Berlin firm of Borsig's. Within a few weeks of the declaration of war, Borsig's men were working in the Ashford shops, erecting these locomotives, the boilers and the frames for which had been sent separately from Germany.

One of the Wainwright's eight P class 0-6-0Ts returned to the town of its birth on 6th June 1992 as part of the ASHFORD 150 celebrations. It was built as no. 753 in 1909. (P.G.Barnes)

6. THE MAUNSELL ERA 1913
Southern Railway 1947 booklet

AINWRIGHT'S successor was R. E. L. Maunsell, first to receive the title of "Chief Mechanical Engineer." Much of his early administration at Ashford was connected with the manufacture of munitions, although he was also engaged in supplying spare and missing parts for Belgian locomotives, made from sketches sent home from the war-ravaged Continent by English and Belgian railway draughtsmen.

The war, however, was not allowed to halt the march of progress at Ashford, and in 1915 the Chemical Laboratory was opened, for the purpose of metal analyses and research into general metallurgical processes. Much later, the scope of this was to be widened, to embrace analyses of coals, oils, paints, and the like.

The first Maunsell locomotives appeared in 1917—big departures from any of the types seen hitherto at Ashford. One class was a mixed-traffic 2–6–0 tender engine; the other, a 2–6–4 express passenger tank, both having outside cylinders, a feature that had been absent from Ashford-built locomotives for many years. And the only saddle tank engine to be found on the Southern Railway at the present time was converted in 1917 by Maunsell from a Wainwright goods engine at Ashford.

An event of importance occurring soon after the return of peace was the introduction of electric welding in the shops.

Then, in 1921, there came a great break with the past with the handing over to the Kent Education authorities of the "railway schools" that had for so many years been not only provided for by the S.E.R. and the S.E.&C.R. but had been so closely linked with the life of the Ashford workpeople.

Finally, with the amalgamation of the railways in 1923, came the day when the last carriage to be built at Ashford rolled out of the shops. Henceforward all carriage work was to be confined to the erstwhile "Brighton" company's works at Lancing and the Eastleigh Works of the other constituent company, the London and South Western.

But Ashford continued to build some very fine engines. In that year of the amalgamation, the Works turned out a batch of three of Maunsell's highly successful "N" class 2–6–0 locomotives. And in 1929 eight of his "U" class engines were to steam their way into service from the Ashford shops.

A fresh development, taking place in 1924, was the establishment of the Physical Laboratory. In close alliance with the Materials

The chemical and scientific side of a big Works is of great importance, not only in testing raw material that reaches the Works, but also for research work.

Inspection Office, experts began to conduct important research work connected with equipment and supplies, and to carry out investigations into the causes of the failure of broken parts. In that year, too, the Works acquired its electro-plating plant, while in 1928 a separate locomotive wheel shop was opened at the south-east end of the Erecting shop, where it could be " fed " by the existing traverser.

An event of 1926 that is remembered was the visit of the present King and Queen—then, of course, the Duke and Duchess of York—who, with Maunsell in attendance to explain the purposes of the machinery and equipment, made a complete tour of the Works, shaking hands with the Foreman in charge of each shop. When the inspection was over and the special train was ready to depart with the visiting party from the Works, it was the Duke, under the supervisory eye of Driver Francis, who opened the regulator of Maunsell's famous Eastleigh-built " Lord Nelson "—at that time the most powerful engine in the United Kingdom—and " drove " the locomotive to Ashford station.

An influx of additional machinery, which included a 35-ton Vaughan overhead crane—now in the New Erecting Shop—occurred between 1929 and 1931, when much of the plant at the recently closed Brighton works was transferred to Ashford. The locomotive shop continued to be the scene of building activity, for there the last examples of Maunsell's 98-ton-odd "N1" class were taking shape.

Ashford Works is proud of a contact with the present King and Queen which dates back to 1926, when as Duke and Duchess of York, they visted the Works. The photo shows them on the footplate of a "Lord Nelson" engine with Sir Everard Baring, the Chairman, Mr.R.E.L.Maunsell, Chief Mechanical Engineer, and Driver Francis.

This was the first of the Maunsell's highly-successful N class engines, built at Ashford in 1917. The design was adopted by the Government in 1924-25 when a number of these locomotives were built at Woolwich to alleviate post-war unemployment.

Then, as the result of the opening of a new depot between the Canterbury and Folkestone lines, the Running (or Engine) Shed adjoining the Machine shop was demolished, and certain railway tracks thus left, became available for the examination of engines prior to their entering the shops. In the same year and the next (1933) locomotive building boomed once again : fifteen Maunsell "N" class came out of the shops, while in 1935 seven large Goods tank engines, Class "W," were built, and three more followed in 1936 —but these were the last complete Southern Railway engines of standard design to be constructed at Ashford. From that date onward —until the 1939–45 war brought, among other less pleasant things, a return to engine building—the resources of the Works were to be devoted wholly to the manufacture of parts and to " general and intermediate repairs."

The year 1937 marked the beginning of a new enterprise for Ashford. Work started on the construction of mechanical parts for

The Smithy Shop and its overhead shafting was photographed in about 1919. The ventilation was improved later.

the Southern Railway's first three oil-electric shunting engines. Four years later similar constructional work was completed for the Railway's first two Main Line Electric Locomotives.

A social occasion that might almost be described as a living memorial to R. E. L. Maunsell—greatly loved and deeply respected at the Works—is the Annual Dinner of the Ashford and District Foremen's Association. From the first assembly held in the winter of 1919 at the George Hotel, in Ashford, Maunsell took the opportunity afforded by the Dinners to reveal to his staff particulars of the programme of work laid down for the months ahead, and these speeches were fraught with such significance for the men (not infrequently haunted by the spectre of " short time ") that the Kent newspapers came to give them the utmost prominence in their columns.

No. 1685 was in a class of its own (S) and had been built in the Works in 1917 using components of a C class goods engine. "D" Box and the station buffet are in the background.

7. THE BULLEID ERA 1937
Southern Railway 1947 booklet

 N 1937 came Maunsell's retirement, and the appointment as Chief Mechanical Engineer to the Southern Railway of Mr. O. V. Bulleid, in whose charge the locomotive, carriage and wagon affairs of the company are resting at the present day. The influence of this original designer upon the company's locomotive and rolling stock policy was to become manifest within a short space of time.

Once again, locomotive building became one of Ashford's accomplishments. The day arrived when even the surprising outlines of Mr. Bulleid's "Austerity" 0–6–0 goods engines grew familiar in the Erecting shops and 14 of the powerful 2–8–0 war-design LMS-type engines for service on that company's system were constructed in 12 months. In addition, a large number of War Department "Austerity" locomotives received overhaul in the shops prior to shipment overseas.

This is the Band that broadcast during the War in the well-known programme "In Town To-night." The picure shows the band in front of the first "Austerity" engine, designed by Mr.O.V.Bulleid, CME, Southern Railway. The name "Austerity" was first applied to the engine by the New York Times. Later on in the was the word was applied to the Ministry of Supply engines.

The Locomotive Erecting Shop during the war. Putting the final touches on the War Department engines for overseas. The whole of the shop is here seen "blacked-out" and artificial light had to be used by day and night.

It is not often that a railway locomotive bears the initials of two different railway companies. This locomotive shows the last locomotive to be built at Ashford Works in the first hundred years. It was of LMS design, but built by the Southern.

Armour plating, mobile workshops, bomb-trolleys, ramp wagons for conveying tanks, tank fittings, and breakdown trains for the U.S. Army, comprised only a part of the essential war material to come out of Ashford Works. With the adaptation of the Wagon Fitting and " Klondyke " shops to an ingenious, progressive system of wagon building, it became possible regularly to produce new goods wagons

Wagons to take supplies to the Eastern front were despatched in kit form. This is the last batch to be sent to Persia. Note the sandbags protecting the gateman's office.

at the really astonishing rate of one vehicle per hour. And in 1941–42 a record was created when 1,600 12-ton open wagons for shipment to Persia were constructed in 12 weeks. Ashford was the first depot in the country to be equipped with a light anti-aircraft gun, which was manned entirely by members of the Southern Railway's own Home Guard unit. Part of the former Royal Train Shed was converted into a Canteen for 360 men and women, and it was from this hall that one heard, on occasion, the B.B.C. broadcast a "Workers' Playtime" programme.

Electric locomotive no. CC1 was recorded under construction in 1941. Two others followed and three diesel-electrics, numbered 10201-3, were built in the early 1950s. Finally a batch of 26 diesel-electric shunters brought locomotive assembly to an end. (Kent Arts & Libraries)

8. ENEMY ATTACK
Vic Mitchell

shford's railway installations suffered as a result of bombing during World War II in six notable events. However, the damage inflicted was much less than that achieved by the RAF on key railway centres in Europe.

A little over a year into the war, sidings near the Hastings line were bombed and a number of tenders stored nearby were damaged on 6th October 1940.

There was a direct hit on the Saw Mills on 30th September 1942, but fortunately fire did not aggravate the situation.

The Machine Shop and Body Shop suffered greatly on 26th October 1942, with the inevitable blast causing havoc to the roofs and windows over a wide area. Two bombs caused the loss of ten lives in the town.

It was a bad autumn for the Works for, on the 27th November of that year, another bomb fell on it, killing one worker. The returning raiders decided on impulse to shoot at a train on the New Romney branch, but one of the two planes was so low that it collided with the dome and chimney of class D3 0-4-4T no. 2365. A further irony was that while the pilot escaped from the crashing aircraft, he subsequently drowned in a dyke. The locomotive crew survived their injuries.

It was on 9th March 1943, that a German reconnaissance plane flying at around 25,000 feet took a photograph of Ashford. It possessed remarkable definition and showed in great detail all the railway installations, the Royal Ordnance complex and other important industrial sites. Barely 40 miles away, on the other side of the English Channel, a Luftwaffe airfield in the Pas de Calais had been established. It was the base of the 10th Squadron of the 54th Fighter Group, led by Oberleutnant Paul Keller, known in the Luftwaffe as "Bombenkeller," for his many low-level attacks over Kent, London and Sussex. No doubt the photograph was used at the briefing of 10/JG 54 on the morning of 24th March 1943.

On that morning, 14 Focke-Wulf 190 fighter-bombers, each armed with 20mm cannon and a 1100lb bomb, took off, pointed their noses in the direction of Ashford and skimmed across the Channel at 300mph, flying below radar cover. On the roof of the railway work's bath-house, in their very basic shelter, two keen-eyed railwaymen, who had undergone a course in aircraft recognition, were on full alert.

At 10.02am they identified the first group of five FW 190s from the most difficult of all angles, a head-on approach at zero feet and a range of three miles. Within seconds railwaymen all over the works were taking cover. Most managed to find some form of protection amid exploding

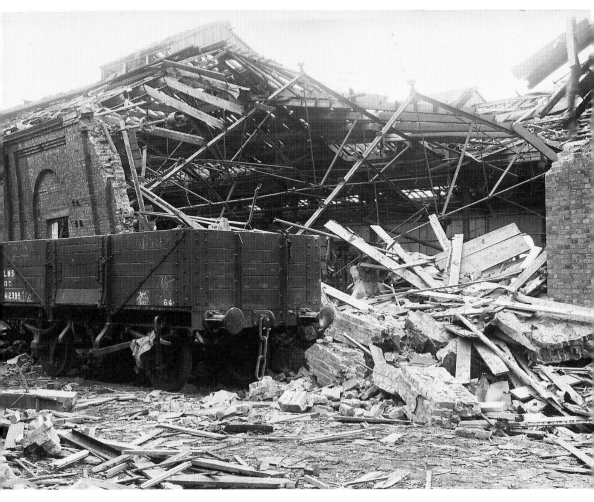

There was severe damage to the Saw Mills on 30th September 1942. (Kent Arts & Libraries)

cannon shells and bombs but some were left exposed to the full might of the air attack.

There was death and destruction at the nearby running shed as a 1100lb high-explosive bomb hit the boiler of E class locomotive no. 1515. Its boiler exploded, adding to the blast of the bomb itself. A second bomb failed to explode. Of the three bombs which fell on the locomotive works, the greatest number of casualties was caused by a bomb which, travelling almost horizontally, skidded off the wheel shop roof, penetrated the end wall of the erecting shop where it shot along for another 100 feet before its delayed action fuse set it off a few feet above ground level.

Eighty-ton locomotives were thrown over like toys; 200 feet of the shop building was destroyed and the casualty list was long. The succeeding groups of planes had to fly around a low hill which threw them off course for the railway works, so they tried to hit the station - one was wide of the mark and a second overshot. The rest, firing several thousand rounds of 20mm shells, dropped their lethal loads around the town centre, causing further heavy casualties and a great amount of damage.

Their prompt activation of the railway works "immediate danger" warning gave their fellow railwaymen a precious 20 seconds to take cover. It also saved the lives of 300 children at the Victoria Road primary school three-quarters of a mile away. Fifty people died in the raid, the worst on a Kent town during World War II. Five of these had been in the works. But it could have been much worse.

Rolling stock standing near the Erecting Shop was damaged by blast on 26th October 1942. (British Rail)

By 1944 the Germans were in retreat and their tactic was revenge bombing with pilotless craft (V1s or "Doodlebugs") or rockets (V2s). Ashford was on the flight path for the V1s aimed at London and some stopped short. On 16th August 1944, damage was caused to stock and signalling north of the works.

Ashford suffered over 4000 air raid alerts between 1939 and 1945.

Some shots of Ashford Works during the war appear in SR's official film "War on the Line", now available from Middleton Press on video.

A crane lifts a wheelset while linemen work up two telegraph poles damaged on 16th August 1944.
(British Rail)

9. ASHFORD WORKS IN 1947
Southern Railway 1947 booklet

This is the year of the centenary of Ashford Works and is to be the last year of the Southern Railway. Both are making great efforts to make good the ravages of war and to overcome the difficulties of post-war shortages of materials.

The works can be proud of its record of 715 new locomotives built and almost 300 rebuilt. Every week, in the locomotive shops, at the present time, some three or four engines receive general overhaul. Simultaneously, intermediate repairs are carried out to another five or six, while in other divisions of the shops work is also going forward on the making of components for locomotives to be erected in shops elsewhere on the Southern. Such members as foundation rings, main frames, frame stretchers and partly machined cylinders are produced at Ashford for " West Country " locomotives—those revolutionary Pacific engines, the creations of the present Chief Mechanical Engineer, which together with his equally famous " Merchant Navy " class, have added on their own a chapter to British railway locomotive history. For these engines, too, Ashford makes complete tenders, of which over 70 have so far been completed. The building, too, of the underframe of a third electric locomotive is proceeding.

While the carriage department is producing machined parts for passenger coaches in course of assembly at Lancing and Eastleigh—and, let it be added, helping to keep the " Southern Electrics " running by renovating twenty or so pairs of motor-bogie wheels every week—the wagon section (apart from the incessant and essential work of repairs) has been turning out new open goods vehicles, over a long period, at the average rate of 55 wagons per 55-hour week.

Incidentally, this productivity has been by no means dedicated selfishly to the interests of industrial transport in the south, for large numbers of wagons have been built to the order of the London and North Eastern Railway. This table shows the quantities of the particular types of wagon constructed in 1946 and indicates the commissioning company in each case :

	No. built in 1946
13-ton mineral (for L.N.E.R.)	90
13-ton open (for S.R.)	600
12-ton covered (for S.R.)	510
40-ton bogie rail (for S.R.)	11
40-ton bogie bolster (for S.R.)	52
16-ton mineral (for L.N.E.R.)	523
Total	1,786

One of the 16-ton all-steel mineral wagons built at Ashford for the London and North Eastern Railway

Mass production - One often hears the phrase "coming off the assembly lines". This photo shows the end of the assembly line for steel wagons which was inaugurated in 1945. The inset shows Mr Barnes, the present Minister of Transport, with Sir Eustace Missenden, the General manager, stencilling the number on a truck prior to its going into service.

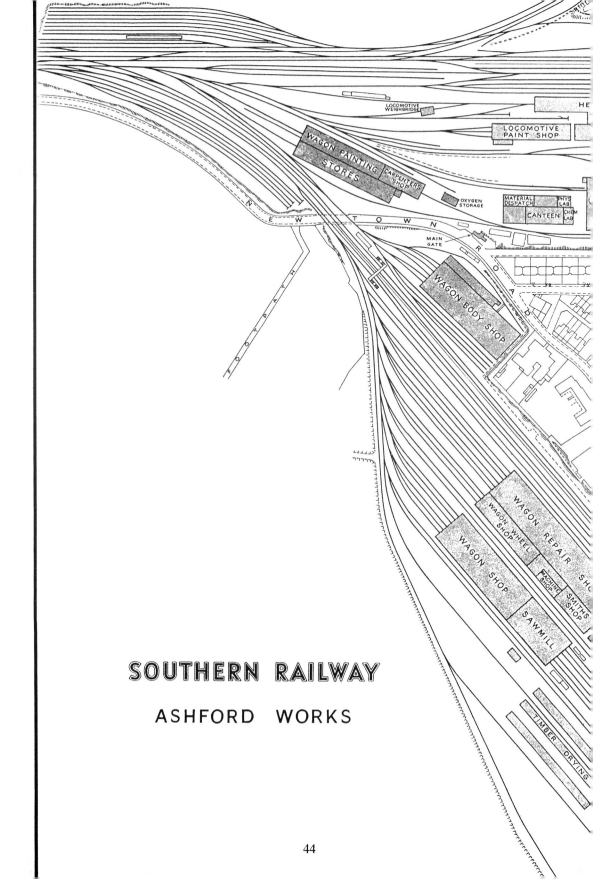

LOCOMOTIVE
WEIGHBRIDGE

HE

LOCOMOTIVE
PAINT SHOP

WAGON PAINTING
STORES
CARPENTERS
SHOP

OXYGEN
STORAGE

MATERIAL
DESPATCH
PHYS
LAB
CHEM
LAB
CANTEEN

MAIN
GATE

N E W T O W N   R O A D

F O O T P A T H

WAGON BODY SHOP

WAGON REPAIR SHOP

WAGON WHEEL SHOP

MACHINE
SHOP

SMITHS
SHOP

WAGON SHOP

SAWMILL

TIMBER DRYING

SOUTHERN RAILWAY

ASHFORD WORKS

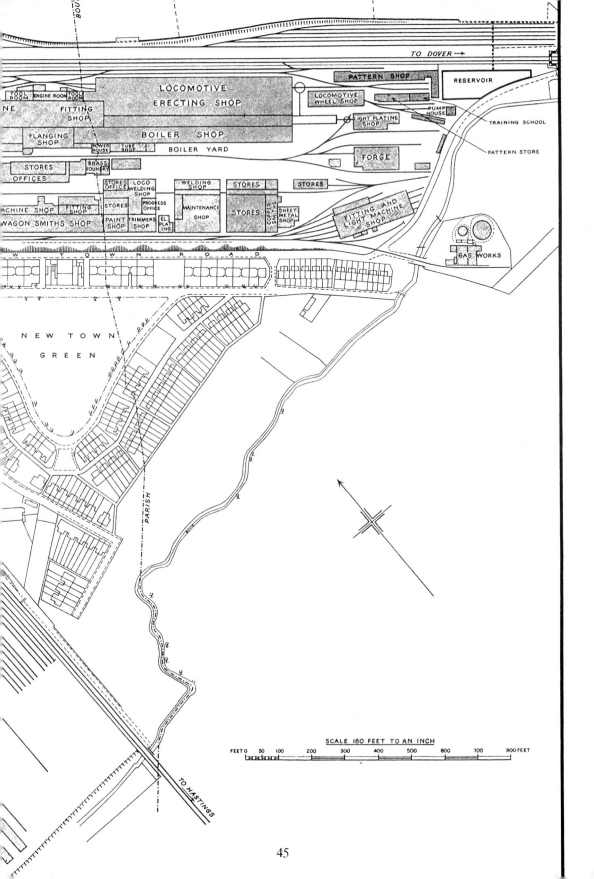

TO DOVER →

LOCOMOTIVE ERECTING SHOP

PATTERN SHOP

RESERVOIR

TOOL ROOM

ENGINE ROOM

TOOL ROOM

FITTING SHOP

FLANGING SHOP

BOILER SHOP

BOILER YARD

POWER HOUSE

TUBE SHOP

BRASS FOUNDRY

STORES OFFICES

STORES OFFICE

LOCO WELDING SHOP

STORES

PROGRESS OFFICE

WELDING SHOP

STORES

STORES

COPPER SMITHS

SHEET METAL SHOP

STORES

MACHINE SHOP

FITTING SHOP

STORES

TEL PLATING

MAINTENANCE SHOP

WAGON SMITHS SHOP

PAINT SHOP

TRIMMERS SHOP

LOCOMOTIVE WHEEL SHOP

LIGHT PLATING SHOP

PUMP HOUSE

FORGE

TRAINING SCHOOL

PATTERN STORE

FITTING AND LIGHT MACHINE SHOP

GAS WORKS

N E W   T O W N   R O A D

NEW TOWN

GREEN

PARISH

TO HASTINGS

SCALE 160 FEET TO AN INCH

FEET 0   50   100   200   300   400   500   600   700   800 FEET

45

The Sawmill, showing the sawdust extractor which has revolutionised sawmills.

The Tyre Furnace in action. Re-tyring locomotive wheels in the Locomotive Wheel shop.

At work in the Physical Laboratory. This important section of the Works was opened in 1924.

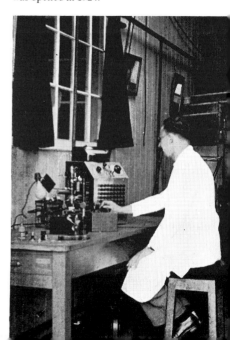

The Erecting Shop in 1947.

Built in 1904, Wainwright's C class 0-6-0 no. 1270 undergoes overhaul in the Erecting Shop in 1947.

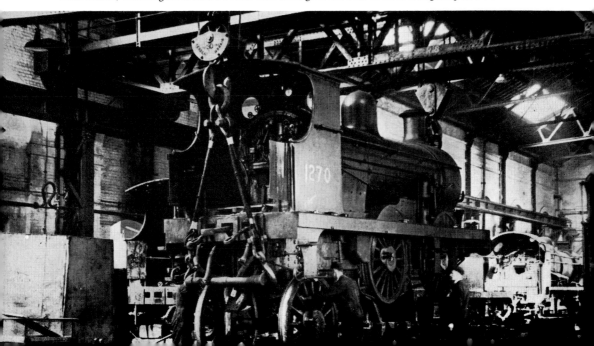

The complete underframe of a 16 ton all-steel wagon in position on a jig, with an hydraulic riveter in action.

Flanging a wagon floor plate in the 135-ton hydraulic press.

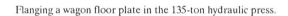

And lately, perhaps just to show that this feat of wagon-building was only a normal, or routine, job, Ashford constructed (again for the London and North Eastern company) a further 977 all-steel 16-ton mineral wagons, at the rate of a wagon an hour.

Needless to say, such a result could have been achieved only by " planning " of the most closely integrated order. Assembly of the underframes of these wagons was made a continuous process, jigs being used throughout. After being mounted on its wheels, each underframe went forward immediately to receive the body, composed mainly of steel plates $\frac{1}{4}$-in. thick. The preparation of these bodies was made quite an independent process. It involved the flanging of 8-ft. wide plates in a three-cylinder 135-ton hydraulic press (made in the Works) and the fitting of pressed steel stanchions by the aid of pneumatic squeeze-riveters. After their arrival in the Body shop, each underframe was furnished with its floor plates, lifted into

At work with pneumatic riveters on a 16 ton all-steel wagon.

position by a mobile crane, and then, in turn, passed over a traverser (also Ashford-made) on to the main assembly line.

Thenceforward, the evolving wagon went through many stages, in the course of which about 800 rivets were applied, more than half of them being driven home by the silent and speedy squeeze-riveting machines. Electric welding, too, played its part in the production of these wagons. Altogether, the whole process was as swift and methodical as it was efficient.

At the same time, heavier all-steel wagons have been under construction, for it has fallen to Ashford to build twenty 40-ton bogie hopper ballast wagons, for the use of the company's Chief Civil Engineer. Vehicles of this type—more intricate in design than the normal four-wheeled standard wagon—have in the past been put out to contract, but Ashford has now shown that there is no need to go farther afield for this kind of wagon.

It remains to speak of certain staff affairs and activities of the present time.

As for many years past, apprentices—themselves, frequently, the sons of former apprentices—are taken into the shops to "serve their time." After completing a term of five years at one trade, they receive a certificate signed by the Chief Mechanical Engineer. There are, in addition, a number of "premium" apprenticeships, offering first-class experience in the Engine Fitting, Machine and Erecting Shops. To-day there are 156 apprentices at the Works ; 143 in the Locomotive department, and 13 in the Carriage and Wagon shops.

Ashford has reason to be proud of its team of 120 trained Ambulance men. From time to time they perform invaluable service to their comrades, on the not infrequent occasions when accidents occur in the shops. The more serious cases are dealt with by a full-time attendant in the specially equipped Ambulance Room. Where necessary, too, a Surgical Aid section assists employees to obtain surgical appliances at reduced cost. Further, practically the whole of the Works staff contribute to a Hospital Fund—founded in 1919 at the instigation of R. E. L. Maunsell. Members of this Fund donated voluntarily £1,900 towards the cost of the New Ashford Hospital.

Of the well-appointed—and efficiently run—National Savings " Selling Centre " it is quite sufficient to say that by its aid a total of *well over* £100,000 has been paid into the national Exchequer. Of many wonderful achievements by this Centre one of the best was for the " *Salute the Soldier Week*," when no less than £23,473 was collected in the converted railway coach standing so modestly outside the principal offices.

Finally, a word on Sport. In 1925 Sir Herbert Walker, the then General Manager of the Southern Railway, opened a Bowling Green and Tennis Courts, towards the initial cost of which the company made a substantial grant. These are situated, together with the Cricket Ground, on railway property near the Works. This Sports Ground provides splendid facilities for recreation to the men and women employed in the shops. Further, there is a Rifle Club and an Angling Club, each with its full complement of enthusiastic members. There can be few industrial centres in the country offering better opportunities for organised sport—and all the social events springing naturally from it—than Ashford Works.

Specialisation. The latest Ashford production, a very specialised wagon for use in re-ballasting the track. Hitherto these wagons have been made by contractors, but Ashford is equipped to make almost anything on wheels.

Ashford has never been behindhand in answering the calls of the nation. During the war "Dig for Victory", Salvage and all other interests were enthusiastically taken up. The photo shows the National Savings "Selling Centre" at which £100,000 has been collected.

10. LOCOMOTIVE SHEDS
Vic Mitchell

ntil 1931, the locomotive running shed was attached to Ashford Works. It is marked *ENGINE HOUSE* on the 1847 plan shown on page 9; its location prior to that is uncertain. It was later lengthened to 200ft and had four parallel roads.

The LCDR had a small engine shed near its terminus but both were closed in 1899. Prior to closure of the former SER shed in 1931, there was an allocation of about 50 locomotives, these including classes C and O1 0-6-0s, H class 0-4-4Ts and various 4-4-0 engines for passenger work. There were sub-sheds at Canterbury West, Maidstone East and West and at Sandgate, although the latter had closed earlier.

Planning of a new shed north of the Dover line commenced in 1927. It was of concrete construction and had ten parallel roads. A 65ft turntable

This is the west end of the running shed in August 1925, with part of the turntable pit in the foreground. The locomotives on the left are D class no. A740 and R class no. A664. "A" stands for Ashford. (H.C.Casserley)

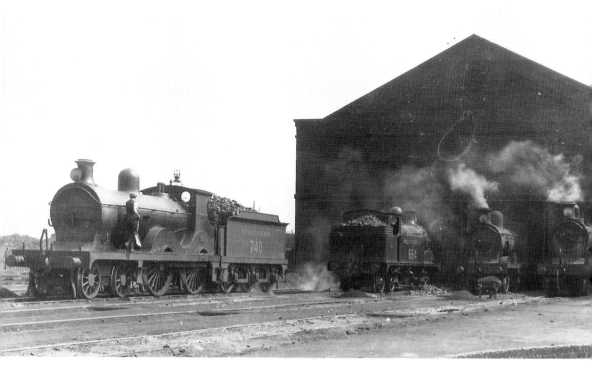

The 1931 running shed is seen in 1960 when its northern three roads were devoted to diesels. Left of centre is the high level roofed coaling stage. (British Rail)

and a covered coal stage were provided in the spacious yard. Although the number of sub-sheds declined, the depot (no. 74A) remained of importance until the decline of steam in the early 1960s. Steam locomotive working ceased in 1963, but a small area of the shed remained in use for servicing diesels until 1968.

Following closure, the South Eastern Steam Centre was established on the site and a substantial number of items of historic rolling stock was collected together on the premises, although part of the roof had to be removed on safety grounds. A subsequent ban on steam movements made the continued operation of the Centre uneconomic. Closure resulted and a protracted dispute followed.

11. ELECTRIFICATION
Vic Mitchell

hile the Gillingham to Ramsgate and Faversham to Dover lines were electrified in 1959, Ashford had to wait until 12th June 1961 for electric trains on the Sevenoaks - Dover route. The Maidstone East - Ashford - Canterbury - Ramsgate services were electrically operated from 9th October of that year.

Power for the electrified lines was supplied at 33000 volts AC by the Central Electricity Generating Board, and fed through oil filled cables to substations, where it was transformed and rectified to 750 volts DC. Twenty three sub-stations, spaced at

Overhead electrification gantries had long gone from most sidings but at Ashford they were still to be seen in 1995, over the berthing sidings near the Hastings lines.

intervals of 3½ miles, had been provided for the first phase of the scheme. About 160 miles of conductor rail, and 87 miles of cable, had been required for the newly-electrified lines.

Rolling stock comprised 53 new four-car units for the fast trains, ten of these having buffet cars, each of which had 17 seats in the dining saloon. An initial batch of 62 two-car units were provided for local services, these having no corridor connections. Ten motor luggage vans were built and fitted with traction batteries so that they could work over non-electrified quayside lines.

For hauling freight trains and also the "Golden Arrow" and "Night Ferry" boat trains, 24 electric locomotives were constructed. Although normally using the conductor rail, they were fitted with pantographs for collecting current from overhead wires fitted in a number of goods yards sidings. These were intended to reduce the danger to railway staff on the ground, but unfortunately some locomotive firemen touched them accidentally with long firing irons.

The new timetable was based on departures from Ashford to London at the following minutes past each hour - 00.18 Waterloo and Charing Cross only, 00.25 Victoria via Maidstone East, 00.27 all stations to Tonbridge where it joined the 00.42 departure which ran non-stop to Paddock Wood and then semi-fast to Charing Cross, 00.48 Victoria via Maidstone East.

The underframes for some of the electric stock were assembled at Ashford Works. Many of the 4VEP (class 423, right) and 4CEP (class 411, centre) units were around 30 years old when this photograph was taken west of the station in October 1995.

12. REBUILDING in the 1960s
Vic Mitchell

he Kent Coast Electrification Scheme envisaged regular dividing and attaching of trains and cross-platform connections between trains on the four electrified routes. To this end the two bay platforms were to be eliminated and replaced by through lines, creating two island platforms.

The main obstacle to this plan was Beaver Road bridge, at the west end of the station. It consisted of four small brick arches, each over one track. A similar structure is still standing at Tonbridge, its limited clearances being evident when a train is passing.

Following the demolition of the bridge and its replacement with long spans, the creation of an entirely new station could proceed. The old station had entrances and brick-built offices on both sides of the railway, two storey on the down (town) side and single on the up platform. The round-headed windows and large key stones gave an imposing appearance.

Photographs of the station before rebuilding can be found in *Redhill to Ashford* (nos. 112, 113, 117 and 118) and the prospective passenger's view of the up side buildings is shown in picture no. 4 in *Branch Lines around Canterbury*.

The new station being flat-roofed with almost fully glazed walls, all architectural styling was lost. A wide footbridge accommodated both a booking office and a buffet. Public access was from the down side only, but a subway was provided to facilitate inter-platform movements. The two through lines were retained for use by boat trains and goods services. Modern materials were used throughout, creating a stark featureless environment. An improved public address system was one notable improvement, as was platform lighting.

S 13747 Ashford Junction Southern Railway Station, Kent

This inter-war postcard view of the east end of the station was little changed when rebuilding started. Both bay platforms are evident. (D.Cullum coll.)

Note the close fit of the coaches in one of the arches of Beaver Road bridge as a Bulleid "Pacific" speeds east with an express in 1957. The main building is above the front coach. (Prof.H.P.White)

Departmental shunter (DS238) stands on the up through road on 9th September 1964 while the frame of the new downside building takes shape. Built in the USA, this was one of 14 similar engines purchased by the SR from the War Department, in 1947. This locomotive is now on the Kent & East Sussex Railway. (H.C.Casserley)

The new buildings on the up island platform were photographed on 6th June 1992 as class 73 electro-diesel no. 73126 **Kent & East Sussex Railway** waits to propel a 4VEP unit to the Chart Leacon Open Day. (P.G.Barnes)

13. RESIGNALLING IN 1962 AND 1984
Vic Mitchell

or over half a century, five mechanical signal boxes had to be manned almost continuously to control the trains passing through or terminating at Ashford. More than one man was necessary for the operation of the largest one at busy times; with rising wages, the running costs became enormous and so an all-electric system controlled from one illuminated panel was introduced in 1962. Mechanical boxes were lettered from west to east thus -

"A" Box. Located on the Maidstone line at the junction with the lines to the former LCDR terminus, this box had 40 levers when it simply controlled the Chatham terminus. Seven more levers were added when the goods connection to the SER opened in 1891. The box was down graded to a ground frame on 22nd September 1929 and was subsequently only manned for goods train movements (see picture no. 115 in *Swanley to Ashford*).

"B" Box. Originally, this 1907 box controlled the junction between the Maidstone and Tonbridge lines by means of 34 levers, these finally increasing to 38. It could be a noisy and smelly location owing to its

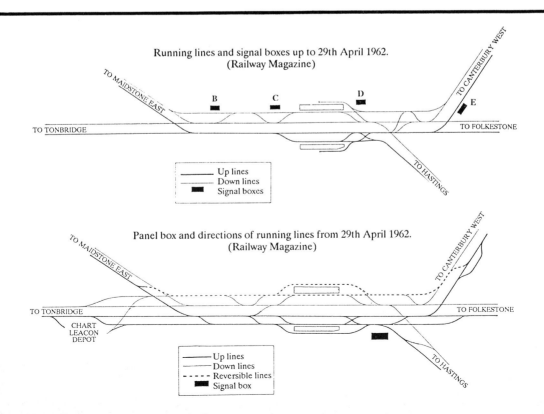

Running lines and signal boxes up to 29th April 1962.
(Railway Magazine)

TO MAIDSTONE EAST

TO CANTERBURY WEST

B   C   D   E

TO TONBRIDGE

TO FOLKESTONE

TO HASTINGS

Up lines
Down lines
Signal boxes

Panel box and directions of running lines from 29th April 1962.
(Railway Magazine)

TO MAIDSTONE EAST

TO CANTERBURY WEST

TO TONBRIDGE

TO FOLKESTONE

CHART
LEACON
DEPOT

TO HASTINGS

Up lines
Down lines
Reversible lines
Signal box

proximity to the cattle market siding (see picture no. 111 in *Redhill to Ashford*). The first box here was called "Maidstone Junction"; it had 20 levers.

"C" Box. This was a busy block post controlling crossovers between the two down lines and the convergence of the two up lines through the passenger station situated a few hundred yards to the east (see picture no. 118 in *Swanley to Ashford*). This 36-lever box dated from 1907 and had been preceded by "Ashford West Yard" box.

"D" Box. The largest box of the group, it controlled the junction of the Hastings line together with all movements at the east end of the station, including both bays and the Works access. The 96-lever box had superseded "Hastings Junction" in 1908 (see pictures 3 and 5 in *Branch Lines around Canterbury*).

"E" Box. Situated between the Canterbury West and Folkestone routes, it controlled the junction between them along with access to the locomotive shed (see picture no. 8 in *Ashford to Dover*). The 77-lever box was built in 1901 as "Ramsgate Junction" and was renamed "E" in 1908 when the number of levers was reduced to 41. There were 56 in use at the time of closure in 1962.

The new panel box came into use on 29th April 1962, eliminating all four Ashford boxes and several rural ones.

In 1984, the track layout was again simplified, to reduce maintenance costs and improve flexibility of operation. The speed limit through the station was increased to 85 mph. The track alterations necessitated extensive modification of the signalling and a new panel was installed. The panel ceased to function on 7th December 1995.

The Dover portion of the 7.35am from Birkenhead has been detached from the Margate coaches on 17th September 1958 and is leaving behind "Schools" class no. 30922 **Marlborough**. "D" Box controlled the operation. (P.Hay)

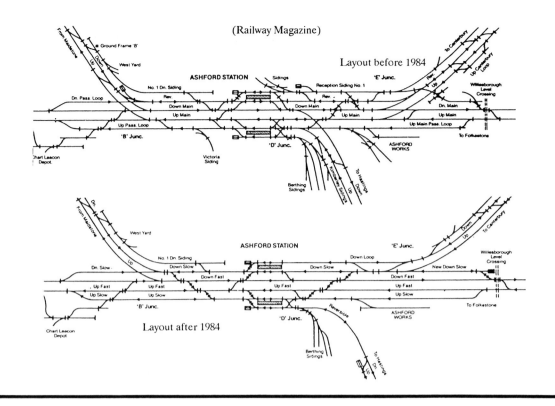

(Railway Magazine)

ASHFORD STATION

Layout before 1984

Layout after 1984

ASHFORD STATION

The 1962 signal box was nearing the end of its life when it was photographed from the new platform 5 on 11th October 1995. Car parks arise in background and the lighting masts reflect in the windows.

14. CHART LEACON in 1992
150th Anniversary Programme

While the coming of the steam railway to Ashford in 1842 led to the growth of Ashford Works as the largest industrial employer in East Kent, it was the coming of Kent Coast electrification that led to the building and future development of Chart Leacon Repair Shop in 1961.

It was the last of five Repair Shops to be built, all of them unique to the Southern Region and its former constituent railway companies; Repair Shops designed for component exchange, overhaul and repair of mechanical and electric components on intensively-used electric multiple units.

In 1984, the remaining Wheelshop activity on the former Ashford Works site together with 40 staff, was transferred to Chart Leacon management. This continued to ensure effective management of some 9000 wheelsets per annum; 6000 at Chart Leacon and 3000 at Ashford Wheelshop for tyre turning and overhaul.

In 1989 Slade Green Repair Shop closed, the site being acquired for the development of the new Networker Depot and the workload being divided between Chart Leacon and Selhurst.

The Repair Shop is 496ft long, 220ft wide and 36ft high. It consists of two duplicate parts, each containing two bays known as North and South side; between them are the centre bays, where wheelset, bogie, brake gear and electrical machine attention is given. The outer bays each span two pitted roads serviced by a pair of 25 tonne overhead travelling cranes. It is in the outer bays that the Depot's outstanding number of rapid vehicle component exchanges and lifting takes place.

Following initial inspection, the unit, usually of four vehicles, is uncoupled, together with all connections between body and bogie. Couplings, brake gear, brake valves and batteries are removed for overhaul along with motor generator, alternator and compressors where necessary. Each vehicle is then lifted onto an adjacent overhauled set of bogies. The eight released bogies (two motor, six trailer) are removed to the east end of the Shop. The vehicles, once lifted over, are mechanically, electrically and pneumatically reconnected and overhauled components fitted followed by preliminary electrical and brake tests.

The released bogies, after dewheeling and traction motor removal from the motor bogies, are cleaned in a wash plant using a caustic, high pressure solution followed by a water rinse. The bogies are then placed on stands, stripped down completely and then rebuilt with refurbished components, before being replaced on a new set of wheels ready for the next unit.

Following the wheelset removal from their bogies, they are stripped of axleboxes and bearings and the axles are examined for cracks and other flaws by ultrasonic testing. The wheelsets can then be turned to regain their original profile on one of the two wheel lathes, or, if retyring and other major repairs are needed, sent to Ashford Wheelshop. Following appropriate attention, the wheelsets are reassembled, greased and stored ready for re-fitting to bogies when required.

Traction motor overhaul provides the major workload of the motorbay at the west end of the Shop. They are placed in manipulators for ease of working where armatures are removed for attention, and field coil and brushgear replacement can take place. Compressors, which supply the air for the braking system, and motor generators or alternators which convert the 750 volt DC supply to a lower control voltage, are also overhauled in the bay.

In the centre bays all small bogie and mechanical components are examined by skilled staff and re-bushed where necessary, while components which are subjected to a high degree of stress are tested for fatigue by a non-destructive method known as Magnetic Particle Inspection (MPI). Gear cases from the traction motors are thoroughly cleaned by a heated vapour solution in large enclosed tanks before being repaired and re-felted. The air-bags which provide the suspension on modern sliding door units are stripped and checked, and springs which

Overhaul work in progress below the gantry crane in South Bay in 1978. (P.Ransome Wallis/NRM)

serve a similar purpose on the older stock are tested and calibrated. Shoe beams and the relevant attachments, which pick up and transfer the track voltage, are also overhauled, as are the intercoach and inter-unit couplings. This section also handles welding and burning, and boasts one of the fast disappearing trades, the blacksmith, who, as well as straightening out damaged parts, carries out rivetting using the modern method of "huck-bolting".

All DC multiple units are fitted with two independent braking systems Electro-Pneumatic (EP), an instantaneous brake made by driver application, and automatic air, which operates automatically should the communication cord be pulled, or by driver application. The valves and controllers which make up these systems are overhauled and tested in the Brake Valve Room which also deals with air-cocks, window wipers and hoses. A separate section is responsible for overhauling the various air pressure gauges associated with braking.

Some units are now undergoing a major electrical overhaul programme whereby re-wiring and replacement of equipment is carried out in the electrical workshop. Large components are re-built and supplied, as are contactors, for making and braking electrical current, and jumpers, which

A dual-voltage class 319 unit (left) was alongside a suburban class 455 unit on 6th July 1991. (M.J.Stretton)

A variety of electric units were on display at the Open Day on 6th June 1992. From left to right a 2BIL, a 4SUB and a 4EPB, all now obsolete. (P.G.Barnes)

provide the electrical connections between coaches. The modification part of the workshop carries out specified modification work to units, the main example at the moment being the fitting of extra dampers to class 455 power bogies, and also overhauls buffet car boilers,toilet hot water tanks and thermostats. Batteries are also overhauled in their separate workshop.

All areas of the Repair Shop are supported by the Tool Room, where specialised machinery work and jigs and fixtures are produced to provide the Depot with a good degree of self-sufficiency.

Alongside the Repair Shop is the four road pitted Inspection Shed, 320ft long by 69ft wide. Initially used for body and electrical inspection associated with unit overhauls, minor unit defects and brake blocking, its role rapidly expanded. The original Ashford Motive Power Depot located east of the station was closed in 1964 and the diesel shunting locomotives and breakdown crane were transferred to the Inspection Shed to add to the allocation of Class 71 DC electric locomotives. Manning of the breakdown train supporting the operation of the 76 tonne crane, and more recently the "Bruff" road rerailing vehicle, was a vital part of the Inspection Shed's activities. A fuel point was built for the fuelling of diesel main line

Also exhibited at the 1992 Open Days was no. E5001, the first of the batch of electric locomotives built for the Kent Coast electrification scheme. (P.G.Barnes)

locomotives and diesel electric multiple units supported by minor examinations and repairs undertaken in the Shed.

Expertise grew on the manning and application of sandite and deicer trains used during the infamous leaf fall season and frosts to maintain the battle for rail adhesion and power respectively. Added to this is the requirement to carry out wagon examination and repairs in the Ashford area, notably during movement of the Channel Tunnel construction trains, or attending traction incidents in a wider geographical area.

In support of the increased workload during the depot's history, material supply has remained vital. Ten thousand stock items now exist, which has led in recent years to the expansion of storage facilities at the south and west end of the depot. The logistics of overhauling and exhanging components (700 items alone on the depot apart from the external contracts), material storage and supply is put into context when up to 12,000 transactions per month can be recorded through the computerised stock control system.   Chart Leacon's main purpose is to carry out planned overhauls (known as C4 Classified Repairs). When the Depot first opened it employed 160 men to carry out overhauls to Kent Coast electric multiple units and diesel electric multiple units based on 100,000 miles frequency intervals. In addition unscheduled repairs such as changing defective wheelsets and traction motors were completed on units between overhauls.

Throughout the 1960s and early 1970s new units were built for Brighton, Bournemouth and Portsmouth services, and the C4 Classified repairs and unscheduled work on these were allocated to Chart Leacon, while the large planned overhauls were allocated to Eastleigh Works (now part of British Rail Maintenance Limited). Electrical overhauls also commenced on 1963-built units in order to improve reliability of the electrical equipment. Modification work to components and vehicles grew. History will probably show that the early 1980s saw the maximum number of vehicles passed through the depot per year - 2,332 C4 overhauls in 1981 and 1,395 unscheduled repairs in 1980, compared with today's figures of 1,700 and 650 respectively.

The 1980s saw further changes that would have impact on Chart Leacon's workload. New units with smaller fleet sizes were introduced with bogies and vehicles capable of running 275,000 miles or more between overhauls. Some of the 1963-built units also demonstrated that their mileage between overhauls could be extended beyond the nominal 100,000 mile intervals. However, this balance of extended mileage leading to reduced overhaul requirements is countered by the level of work now demanded by the customer of the modern overhaul to ensure that maximum mileage can be reached between overhauls.

The Depot holds a proud record of the highest Classified Repair production output by volume and lowest downtime per unit class of any British Rail location. This led directly to the "Chart Principle" being used as the "role model" for the Board's Cost Effective Maintenance Policy at other overhaul sites in 1986.

Chart Leacon staff, some of whom are long serving railwaymen who started in Ashford Works, are infinitely proud of their history and, to quote the new motto, wish to continue in the same vein - "Beavering Away!"

Chart Leacon Level 5 Depot is one of the largest users of computer based information technology on British Rail. Currently, 60 computer terminals are used by office and workshop staff in the day to day running of the Chart Leacon Repair Shop site and Ashford Wheelshop.

Many of the terminals can access the three mainframe computers located in Derby, Crewe and Nottingham, providing a link to the many and vast computer systems used by BR nationally and identified by equally ingenious acronyms such as LOVERS, RAVERS, TOPLS, PADS, IMACS, PEARLS, IBIS AND AXIS.

Chart Leacon is one of the largest users of RAVERS (RAil VEhicle Records System) in terms of the number of component exchanges carried out during the overhaul of vehicles throughout the year.

With the constant endeavour made to update, improve and expand both hardware and software, the capability and expertise is there to design and implement tailor-made systems.

One example of this is the recently introduced WheTS (Wheelset Tracking System) from which it is possible to locate wheelsets both at Chart Leacon and Ashford Wheelshop, identify and monitor their repair status and subsequently control and record which vehicle they are finally fitted to. This gives the production staff real-time control of the wheelsets being overhauled, giving great savings in manpower and money.

The replica **Rocket** ran at Chart Leacon in June 1992, serving as a reminder of events over 150 years earlier in the North of England. (P.G.Barnes)

15. THE WHEELSHOP in 1992
150th Anniversary Programme

shford Wheelshop employs 45 staff. The workload consists mainly of wheelsets from Electric Multiple Unit (EMU) vehicles, primarily from Chart Leacon, but wheelsets are also received and despatched to other depots. In addition, Ashford Wheelshop also contracts to overhaul wheelsets on behalf of Rolling Stock private owners. The most notable example of this type of work has been the overhaul of wheelsets for the Foster Yeoman privately owned Class 59 locmotives.

In a typical year, Ashford Wheelshop will overhaul around 3000 wheelsets. The Wheelshop can overhaul all types of wheelsets, but there are two basic types. They are the tyred wheel, and the monobloc wheel. The roadwheel of a tyred wheel comprises a steel tyre which is shrunk onto a centre. The two roadwheels are then pressed onto axles to form the wheelset. Monobloc wheels have no tyres, the roadwheels being a single solid unit.

The usable life of both tyres and monobloc wheels is between five and seven years, NSE EMUs covering between a half million to a million miles in this time, depending on the vehicle type.

When a tyred wheel wears, it can be refurbished by heating the old tyre in a gas fired ring until it expands to allow removal from the centre. After both tyres are removed, the centre diameters are measured and new tyres are bored to fit the centres. The new tyres are then heated to 300 degrees C, and the centre lowered in. The assembled wheels are then machined to ensure the wheelset negotiates both plain track and points in a safe manner. All wheelsets are dynamically balanced to ensure a smooth ride.

When a monobloc wheel wears, the old wheel must be pressed off the axle. This is done using a hydraulic press, exerting a force of (typically) 85 tons. New wheels are then bored and are pressed onto the axle. No further machining is required, but, again, the wheelset will be balanced prior to despatch.

Periodically, all wheelsets have the axles tested using ultrasonic testing techniques. This can detect the early signs of a flawed axle. If an axle fails an ultrasonic test, Ashford Wheelshop will remove the wheels (using the press), and then determine whether the axle can be reclaimed. Axles can be reclaimed by placing the axle in a centre lathe and cutting grooves to remove any flaws. If the axle cannot be reclaimed, a new axle is machined from a steel blank, with critical areas (such as seats for wheels) being precision ground to a fine finish. The existing wheels are then pressed onto the axle and the axle is ultrasonically tested.

Recently turned wheelsets stand near the turntable on 29th April 1991. (B.Morrison)

The majority of electric trains running on Network SouthEast have four powered wheelsets. The powered wheelsets in a train have two extra components - a gearwheel, through which the power of the electric motor is transmitted to the wheels, and a suspension tube. The suspension tube supports some of the weight of the electric motor, and consists of a tube, through which the axle runs, supported on roller bearings. These components are also press fitted onto the axle and overhauled as required at Ashford Wheelshop.

Closure of the Ashford Wheelshop was announced in 1993.

16. BUILDING PRESERVATION
Roger Airey

The first SER station built at Ashford was, we understand, a typically wooden affair which only survived for about twenty years, and was situated slightly nearer to France than the existing one. The new platform canopies were supported by stanchions which bore the name of W.Richards and Co Leicester and were dated 1908. An attempt was made to retain these, nine trusses being on each platform together with the lattice work girders connecting them.

When work started on the International Passenger Station (IPS) in May

The gate house and the clock tower, along with the water tower were still standing in October 1992. Beyond are the then recently replaced round-headed windows. (V.Mitchell)

1994, a fascinating collection of buildings stood in the former Up Yard. These had been occupied by the Permanent Way Dept and their concrete walls and asbestos roofs hid a rather lavish interior. The main rooms were panelled in wood half way up the walls, and cast iron radiators heated the building. At either end of the complex could be seen weather boarded cabins which had obviously been brought on to the site from elsewhere. One was destroyed to make way for a diverted gas pipe, but the other was preserved. This, was the wooden-framed slate-roofed top of the signal box preceeding Ashford "B" or "C" Box or possibly Folkestone East. This small traditional and delightful building was dismantled at the eleventh hour by a dedicated team from the East Kent Light Railway and, in due course, will form their tea room.

John Laing (the contractors) agreed to save the Little Engine Shed on

SECR coach no. 2947 in aerial transit in August 1986. (E.Graves)

The tall boiler shop and much of the remainder of the Works were still standing as four class 47 diesels raced towards Dollands Moor, where they would collect more freight from mainland Europe. (V.Mitchell)

the down side of the former station. This was an undistinguished grey corrugated iron clad and roofed building, its five massive girders indicating that, at one time, it was an industrial building of some importance; the key to its former use being in the smoke vent along the ridge of its roof. Laing's were supported by a team from the Kent & East Sussex Railway at Tenterden in their efforts to dismantle and transport it from the site.

The small former Pay Office, also on the down side, was whisked away one weekend and can now be found safe and secure at the Elham Valley Railway Trust's museum complex at Peene near Newington, just behind the Channel Tunnel Terminus at Cheriton.

Thus three buildings were saved from the IPS site but much was lost, including the original 1870 SER stables which were replaced by a Portacabin. Destruction of our railway architecture started in World War II when the Works were bombed on several occasions and various buildings were totally or partially destroyed. Observers were posted on the top of the Bath House on New Town Green. A huge tank was on its roof but this was removed when the building, now called Cubit House, was converted into eight flats. In the top two flats the massive cast iron beams that supported the tank can still be seen.

When I first visited Ashford in the early 1970s, a pair of charming Italiaite style cottages could still be seen in Newtown Road, complete with a goat in the front garden. These cottages, built by the same architect that designed Rye station, were the sad remains of four pairs of railwaymen's cottages built (one assumes) at the time of the opening of the Hastings Line. Their fragmented remains now lie beneath the IPS station and access road.

The West Yard or Chatham terminus station lost its engine shed after the preserved Stirling Class O1 moved to the South Eastern Centre, in the former Motive Power Depot in Hunter Avenue, close to the famous Willesborough Level Crossing, the only manually operated crossing between London and Paris. The water tower and turntable at the West Station must have gone at the same time, a great loss.

The nine-road Kimberley shed adjacent to and west of the Hastings line stood derelict for many years after being damaged by fire and hooligans. The site was later used to store Channel Tunnel concrete linings; a siding was relaid and a gantry crane was installed.

The six-road Kimberley Carriage shed survived a few more years. It was a fine Victorian industrial building with 33 cast iron columns supporting 66 wrought iron roof trusses. This had been the Works saw mill and paint shop; timber was stacked in open sided wooden sheds so it would season. A car breaker set up business in this building and stacked his compressed car bodies four high, such was the height of the roof. A small fire destroyed one bay and this was given as the reason to demolish this fine building. Laings have more recently recycled the concrete floor, crushing it to make hardcore and placing it on the many car parks around the IPS site, including the former football pitch in New Town Road.

The most dramatic loss was the Royal Train Shed which stood just inside the main gate beside the listed Clock Tower and Kiln Cafe. Used as the works canteen in its final years, this historic building was also listed. However, it vanished one weekend.

The Motive Power Depot had a ten-road shed and seven roads were lifted in around 1974 when the South Eastern Steam Centre ran into difficulties due to not being allowed to move any of the 12 steam locomotives that had found a home there.

To many local residents the loss of the Bath Meadow Cricket Ground was the biggest blow they had to suffer for the sake of the IPS multi-storey car park in New Romney Marsh Road. Owned by the British Railways Staff Sports and Social Club, this river-side cricket wicket was quite delightful on a Sunday afternoon in summer when matches were played on its well manicured green sward.

The Royal de Lux, latterly known as The Picture House, was also swept away to make room for the new roundabout on the seven mile route from Junction 9 on the M20 to the International Station. Behind the cinema stood the original SER station master's detached house in a fine imposing Victorian style. This stood semi-derelict and roofless for many years after a railwayman had bought it from his employers and sold it to an insurance company. In its back garden was a wonderful ancient pear tree, not unlike one of those five branched candle sticks; this survived a few months longer than its former owner's period house.

The Steam Power Saw Mills on the down side were demolished as were the workshops; these even boasted a short narrow gauge track to handle the baulks of timber. On the site a large number of old signs were found including Margate Sands and Ramsgate Harbour, stations that closed as long ago as 1926. Sadly a World War II style Bailey bridge was also cut up in spite of pleas to leave it where it was, spanning the river beside an alder tree.

Plans to obtain a small tank engine from the National Railway Museum to place on a plinth on the down side domestic station may come to fruition. It is, I feel, worth recording that an attempt was made to create a visitor attraction amongst the sea of car parks .

The design of the IPS is said to have been inspired by the new station at North Woolwich and the De la Warr Pavilion at Bexhill. The author of these few words always felt it had been inspired by a London tram, its rounded ends being the clue, but on hearing of the Woolwich connection, the truth dawns, our IPS is surely based on the twin funnelled Woolwich Steam Ferries.

When British Railways decide to renovate an historic building which they inherited from the private sector, they usually make an extremely good job of it; two local examples come to mind.

The Wheelshop was closed in 1994 and all the ancient and modern milling machines and lathes were taken away. The building, however, was converted into plush offices for Railtrack staff. The round headed windows, taken out about twenty years ago and replaced with ugly concrete lintels, were removed and, using yellow stock bricks from the Long Shop, the original-style mid-19th century windows have been replaced.

The Royal Commission for Ancient Buildings (themselves now housed in the former offices of the Great Western Railway Works at Swindon) produced an excellent report on Ashford Railway Works, and came to the conclusion that they were unique and should be preserved in their totality. With the restoration of the Wheel Shop, complete with its original timber truss roof and Princess Tie Rods, one feels that a step has been taken in this direction.

Another Victorian building recently restored by Infrastructure Building Services of the former BR is the old bacon factory in Victoria Road. Here an ugly steel lintel and steel shutter were taken away and the moulded brickwork replaced to match the original. The Kent peg tiles were carefully removed from the little curving gables and taken away to be reused. Slates replaced the peg tiles at the bacon factory and look in keeping with the Edwardian style. Pledge's flour mill adjacent to this building was, for many years, owned by BR who rented it to the Pledge family, but after around sixty years decided that nothing would ever happen on this land near the station, so they sold it. Sadly this fine Victorian mill burnt out in September 1994, the brick shell some 18 inches thick being declared unsafe by the Borough Council.

Ashford must be the only town in the south-east to still have a station that closed to passengers as long ago as 1899, when the London Chatham and Dover Railway joined forces with their rivals, the South Eastern Railway. This terminus station was converted into to four flats some years ago, but form the perfect site for a Railway Museum/Library.

In November 1985, four LCDR carriage bodies were discovered by a builder in a wooden bungalow with a corrugated iron roof at 188 Kingsnorth Road in South Ashford. The builder generously gave them to the Kent and East Sussex Railway. A few days later a party gathered in the little 1920s building armed with screwdrivers and started work. I found myself in the kitchen, a small room, but complete with sink, cooker etc. However, after two hours it became apparent that I was no longer in a humble kitchen, but was, in fact, in the guard's compartment of an elderly Victorian railway carriage, complete with his ducket for looking down the side of the train. Four carriage bodies (nos. 2947,3022,3062 and 3361) had been used in the bungalow's construction, arranged with a corridor down the centre. All the outer doors and windows were still in situ; two carriages had most of their sides removed to make larger rooms.

Only two of the Chatham bodies were considered restorable at Tenterden. One compartment was saved from a third body but the rest of the teak framing was broken up. No. 2947, built in Ashford Works in 1901 to the LCDR design was placed on a luggage van underframe and fully restored to traffic on the Kent & East Sussex Railway in August 1995.

17. STEAM REVIVAL
Roger Airey

 n the summer of 1986, Chart Leacon celebrated its 25th birthday. The star exhibit was King Arthur class 4-6-0 *Sir Lamiel* no. 777. This was, I believe, the first steam locomotive to appear in Ashford for thirty or so years, since the Total Steam Ban (TSB) had been imposed. The open day was a great success and drew a large number of visitors which may have proved to British Rail that such events are very good public relations exercises.

Behind *Sir Lamiel,* on a long siding, were three bogie brake vans in which rides were offered to visitors for a round trip up and down the length of the yard, all proceeds going to the Woking Homes. Sadly one of the connecting rods was bent due to priming, and a couple of hours were lost whilst the home based skilled craftsmen took off the heavy rod and straightened it. It took about five of them to lift it back on, meanwhile visitors were allowed up onto the footplate.

However, in 1990 it was decided to celebrate the Battle of Britain 50th anniversary and since "Battle of Britain" class steam locomotive no. 34027 *257 Squadron* was nearing the completion of its restoration, it was decided to rename this engine at Folkestone Central. It was even suggested that this engine would haul a train up the Harbour line, but then somebody decided that the swing bridge, which had not swung for many years, would not take the weight.

On the appointed day in June, Class 73 *Kent and East Sussex Railway* piloted *257Squadron* down to Folkestone West and here a most remarkable event took place. A NSE staff manager seeing so many photographers waiting at Folkestone Central, decided on his own initiative to have the Class 73 taken off, to permit the steam loco a free passage into Folkestone Central. This turned out to be an historic first, the first time in thirty years that a fare paying steam hauled train had run on the third rail system.

Having disappointed a great many people by not allowing a steam hauled Boat Train to run down to Folkestone Harbour in 1990, NSE must have felt obliged to lay on such an event in 1991. Shepway Council were also planning a Festival, so a railway historic ride would become part of their overall scheme.

"West Country Class" *Taw Valley* and Class 4 2-6-4T no. 80080 were the pair of steam locomotives that arrived to push and pull the Boat Train up and down the steep Harbour line over two days. They were stabled in Ashford at Chart Leacon, where they could be coaled and watered away from prying eyes.

Knowing that Swindon and Woking had both celebrated 150's, it dawned on me that we might do the same in November 1992. Sir Bob Reid had just replaced Robert Reid as Chairman of British Railways, so it was an excellent moment to write and congratulate him on his new part time position and invite him down to Ashford in 18 months time to join in our 150th railway birthday party.

A reply duly arrived from Waterloo Station, thanking me for my letter and saying that they would consider such an event. This was quickly followed up by a letter suggesting that they do more than think about planning it; I suggested steam hauled trains to Hastings across the Romney Marsh via Rye. Another letter arrived from a weary NSE official, bringing the good news that such an event would take place in June 1992.

So "Ashford 150" came into being, the Borough Council even decided to support the event to the tune of £15,000. Chart Leacon would again open its doors to the public as it had in 1986. I felt something ought to take

"King Arthur" class no. 777 **Sir Lamiel** was a popular feature at Chart Leacon in June 1992. Behind it is BR class 4 4-6-0 no. 75069 and its support coach. (P.G.Barnes)

place down in the Works, after all this was where history was made in the form of 639 steam engines in the period 1847-1962. I went down to talk to the man in charge of the Wheel Shop, he was keen to lay on an exhibition in spite of the bleak future of this small cog in BR's vast engineering arena. The Crane Workshop which was housed in the former main Erecting Shop was also willing to put on a display. Meanwhile the Council had come up with the idea of a Victorian Fair on Newtown Green adjacent to the Works. Chart Leacon went to town and built a temporary station so that rail born visitors could take a shuttle from the station. This crude platform they named "Ashford International", the future of which at that time still seemed in doubt.

The Wheelshop manager excelled himself and had his skilled staff make 500 miniature brass wheel sets to sell for charity. The atmosphere in the cleaned up Wheel Shop was very good as the period building had not been altered for a great many years; its roof still boasted "Princess Rods".

Taw Valley and no. 75069, paintings of which hang proudly in the Mayor's parlour here in Ashford, were the locomotives that would haul a train to Hastings over the weekend of the 6th-7th June. The weekend before, a special party had been invited up to London Bridge to witness the naming of class 33 no. 33114 as *Ashford 150*. They duly arrived, a little worse for wear, back at Ashford Station and were then taken by bus down to Newtown Green to officially launch the Victorian Fair. The loco only survived about nine months, but the Fair continues without any railway input of any kind, although in 1993 there was a Model Railway exhibition in the Wheelshop which was due to close the following year.

The steam locomotives took it in turns to haul the train to Hastings and whilst one was in action the other stood in the Erecting Shop. A one-third scale model traction engine puffed up and down filling the air with steam and smoke thus convincing anybody who was in doubt that this really was a steam locomotive workshop. Until seven bays were removed from the station end of this Victorian building, it was said to be the longest railway workshop in the country; indeed it was known as The Long Shop.

The steam trains ran back and forth on Saturday and Sunday, full most of the time, a great feeling of pride and well being built up at the station. For me the most memorable scene was on the Sunday evening. *Taw Valley* with its fare paying passengers aboard its maroon coloured coaches was about to depart for London, the first steam-hauled train to carry passengers on the route in thirty years. The safety valves were lifting and steam bounced off the underside of the road bridge covering all and sundry, and whilst we all thoroughly enjoyed this spectacle in came no. 75069, its support coaches forming an unofficial second train back to the "Smoke". So for a few precious minutes two steam locomotives stood side by side at the London end of platforms 1 and 2 at Ashford Station, an act not since repeated.

No. 34027 *Taw Valley* pulled away first with the second train following closely behind; what a grand sight they must have made for lineside train

"Merchant Navy" class no. 35028 **Clan Line** takes the down through line on 27th May 1995 as it speeds past temporary screens on platform 3.

watchers as they dashed back to London Bridge. Dusk was falling by this time.

Ashford 150 was a huge success. £11,000 was raised at Chart Leacon for Woking Homes; £3,000 was taken in the Wheelshop and Erecting Shops, even without any pre-publicity. Rail News reported that a profit of £42,000 had been made running the steam specials to Hastings.

As I recall it the year 1993 was rather disappointing with only one steam special passing through Ashford on an evening in January. This was *Britannia* disguised as *William Shakespeare*, one of only two of the "Britannia" class to survive, the other being *Oliver Cromwell*.

On 7th May 1994, at about 5am I heard what sounded like a wheel slip and shunting noises with a steam engine. At first I imagined I was dreaming and then I realised that it was real. A pair of Standard Class 4 tank engines (nos. 80079 and 80080) had arrived at Chart Leacon for watering and coal, ready to run down to Folkestone to once again haul a boat train on the steep 1 in 30 Harbour line. For several minutes, as the birds sang their dawn chorus, these two engines shunted their support coaches and positioned themselves at either end of their Boat Train. It was a very pleasant awakening.

At about midday no. 70000 *Britannia* (disguised this time as *Iron Duke)* was due to haul the special Channel Tunnel opening train. Several locals had heard and were waiting behind the cattle dock gates in the market. Seeing people waiting for something, others joined the queue that soon stretched all the way along the gates. By the time the steam hauled train appeared, about three hundred were waiting to see it pass. Many cameras clicked and children were held up to wave; most had never seen a steam loco on the main line before. Once upon a time two trains from Romney Marsh arrived here every week with cattle.

The number of steam hauled trains in 1995 almost doubled those of previous years. On March 18th, *Clan Line* no. 35028 made her first appearance of the year. This preserved loco has been fitted with air brakes so that she can haul modern coaching stock. A steam operated air compressor has been fitted in the rear of the tender. Sadly on her first run the flexible pipe broke and she had to tow a class 47 Diesel just to operate the new braking system.

Clan Line appeared (without the diesel) again on the 20th May, this time hauling the Venice Simplon Orient Express coaches, including *Lucille* which is owned by a local Ashfordian. She returned at speed passing the footbridge by the market at a good 60mph, a sight to savour for some time. *Clan Line* made similar excursions through Ashford on 27th May and 23rd September 1995. As all the turntables have been cut up for scrap, steam hauled trains turn left at Ashford for Canterbury and go on down to Minster, turn right and then return via Deal and Dover with the engine still at the front.

With the opening of the International Passenger Station, much revenue could be raised with the operation of regular steam hauled trains to Hastings, as happened one weekend in 1992.

To end this chapter of steam it would, I feel, be an excellent place to record the few surviving steam engines that were "constructed" (never built or assembled) at "Ashford Locomotive Establishment".

Class	Wheels	No.	Year	Location
D	4-4-0	737	1901	National Railway Museum
P	0-6-0T	27	1910	Bluebell Railway
P	0-6-0T	178	1910	Bluebell Railway
P	0-6-0T	323	1909	Bluebell Railway
P	0-6-0T	556	1909	Kent & East Sussex Railway
H	0-4-4T	263	1905	Bluebell Railway
O1	0-6-0	65	1896	Kent (Private site)
U	2-6-0	1625	1929	Mid-Hants Railway
U	2-6-0	1638	1931	Bluebell Railway

18. REBUILDING 1995
John Laing Plc

T he £50m joint venture with British Rail was a landmark project for the Laing Group. It followed the Government's private finance initiative, with Laing taking responsibility for cost and risk in return for a passenger usage fee from the end user, European Passenger Services, formerly a subsidiary of British Rail.

The Laing Civil Engineering team on site made rapid progress with the new international station, and construction of a new domestic railway station for Railtrack and South Eastern Train Operating Company (SETOC). The project also included a major multi-storey car park, plus four ground-level car parks.

Travel to the continent on the Eurostar is only available via the International Station at Ashford or by using Waterloo Station. Ashford is an international gateway for passengers travelling to Europe, especially those wishing to use their cars right up to the point of departure. The aim is to compete with the terminals at London's airports. Ashford offers people safe, secure and reliable parking facilties so that they can use the Eurostar link with confidence and convenience.

There were three phases to the project being carried out on the site of the existing Ashford station. Two existing central platforms were extended to serve Eurostar trains. They are international land space and not legally in the UK, rather like being airside at an airport terminal.   The International Passenger Station has full passport control and border entry facilities including customs and immigration.

The new footbridge and temporary entrance is seen in October 1994. The booking office and buffet were on the old part of the footbridge. (M.J.Stretton)

Platforms 5 and 6 were well advanced on 22nd October 1994, as were the new buildings on the international platforms and the foundations for the emergency evacuation footbridge. (V.Mitchell)

Phase I involved extending the old down island platform for Eurostar trains and building a new island platform further north. Phase I was split between Laing and other contractors.

Phase IA contract was let by Railtrack to Geoffrey Osborne, and involved platform extensions for the IPS, building two more for the domestic station, also structural steel for canopies over the platforms, as well as bridges to the IPS.

The Laing part was Phase IB, which involved platform building and fitting them out with curtain walling, lighting, heating, tiling and finishings. The other Phase I works, including new tracks, signalling and associated works, were carried out by Railtrack.

Phase II was the International station itself with access road and forecourt, as well as the domestic station and ground level car park with 1000 spaces. Project manager Simon Lander said: "In this phase, all works north of the railway are associated with the domestic station, and all those south are part of the International station".

Both international and domestic stations were fitted out to a high architectural standard, with a cool, sophisticated look to walls and ceilings, high quality lighting and fittings, stainless steel finishes, plus deep blue painted structural steel, emphasising the structural form and large glazed areas. The overall look is more akin to airport terminals and departure lounges than traditional railway stations, with the aim of attracting more international business travellers.

Phase III involved creating 2000 car park spaces through a high specification, multi-storey car park and construction of ground level car parks.

Work started in June 1994 on the first section of the contract, the International Passenger Station, with other sections beginning as other parts of the site were handed over during a seven-month period.

Phases II and III were planned for completion in December 1995 while Phase IB was to be ready by August. In fact, the team handed over car park A several months ahead of schedule. Car park B, its access road, a roadbridge and a footbridge, were handed over in January 1995, eleven months ahead of schedule.

Groundworks and structural steelworks on the domestic station were finished and the team heading for a completion date in August 1995, tying in with railway works moving from platforms three and four to five and six, and completion of the Phase IB works. At 412m, the international platforms are much longer than the domestic platforms, in line with the extra long Eurostar trains which are 392m long.

The multi-storey car park was finished to a high specification with closed-circuit television and painted ceilings, good lighting and 24-hour security monitoring.

Laing declared that "the primary driving force is that people feel comfortable leaving their cars there while they are travelling. It's in our interest as the developer to make sure the maximum number of passengers use the facilities because of the revenue arrangement". The same approach applied for the ground level car parks for longer stay parking. "The major difference about working on this project is that because we are funding it we have control of the specifications and the design. It's given us much more responsibility, but also much more control. Because it's our money we are very conscious of spending it wisely".

A June 1995 view from the lighting tower (seen in the previous picture) shows the international terminal on the left and the international platforms in the centre. The guitar shaped structure (right) is the entrance for passengers for South East Trains. Plans show Union Railway's route running parallel to platform 6 and a further rebuilding of Beaver Road bridge. (Railtrack)

The company concluded "Ashford was an exciting and important project for the Laing Group. It was the first privately-developed railway station in the UK for many years and was one of the first schemes under the Government's private finance initiative".

A new road system was constructed and a footbridge for car park users was built in Autum 1995. Outgoing passengers use a footbridge to reach platforms 3 and 4, while those returning from Europe have an exclusive subway to the terminal building. (V.Mitchell)

The new domestic booking office appears to be partly roofed with an aircraft wing. Although further from the town centre, the entrance is served by frequent minibuses. (V.Mitchell)

19. RESIGNALLING IN THE 1990s
Richard Bosworth
© Signalling Control U.K. Ltd.

n 1984, the track layout at Ashford was simplified to improve flexibility and reduce maintenance costs. The new layout was controlled from the Entrance / Exit panel in the existing signal box using a new Route Relay Interlocking with Electronic Route Setting Equipment (ERSE) housed in an extension to the old relay room, which was stripped of its obsolete equipment.

This layout and signalling remained more or less unchanged until 1994 when the first modifications to accommodate alterations for the Channel Tunnel Project were undertaken.

The advent of the opening of the Channel Tunnel created the need for upgrading and remodelling much of the existing Railway from London to the Tunnel and the creation of complete new Installations and Depots to service the new rolling stock and to provide secure marshalling yards for the new passenger and freight services which would use the Tunnel.

The Resignalling and Remodelling associated with this huge project was nominally split into two areas, namely London End and Country End and covered the routes from Waterloo, via a new flyover linking the South East lines to Victoria with the South West lines to Waterloo (where a new International Station was built), to Ashford and Folkestone. Through the Country End, there are two main routes to Ashford, one via Tonbridge (Channel Tunnel Route One) and one via Maidstone (Channel Tunnel Route Two).

The extent of all these alterations meant extensive stagework alterations to the signalling system which was managed in two separate ways.

Firstly, the signalling equipment at the London End was comparatively young, therefore the existing Panel for Victoria Signalling Centre was altered along with its Remote Relay Rooms. In respect of the London End at Waterloo, the changes were incorporated into the Waterloo Area Resignalling Scheme and a new Relay Room was provided for Waterloo which is controlled from Wimbledon Panel.

Secondly, in respect of the Country End works, due to the age of the existing equipment and the large changes needed to many Signal Boxes, Relay Rooms etc., it was decided to control the Country End from a new Integrated Electronic Control Centre (IECC) located at Ashford. This would centralise the control of the main routes through Kent to the Tunnel.

Due to many different proposals over the exact remodelling and

High security fencing surrounds the IECC. On the right is one of the Travelling Post Office vehicles that run to Manchester overnight. (V.Mitchell)

facilities needed at Ashford, it was removed from the main scheme and treated as a separate project in its own right. Meanwhile the IECC was constructed and the first areas of the Country End were commissioned onto it in early 1993

In order to facilitate the change from the existing layout at Ashford to the final, a staging strategy was developed to manage the transition. This took into account the station reconstruction work and had to be co-ordinated closely with this work to ensure minimum interference and upheaval to passengers.

The preferred method of commissioning by the Engineering Contractors was for a single closure over an extended period, but this was not possible because of the heavy traffic through Ashford and the fact there is no alternative route to Dover and the Channel Tunnel over which traffic could be diverted. It was decided that a number of smaller stages would be adopted where smaller areas of track circuits and points would be converted to final circuitry, but fed in parallel to the existing Signal Box. In addition to the large number of P.Way Stages, where "like-for-like" or new points were installed, there were two partial closures, one at Easter and one in late Summer 1995.

The last major stage in the P.Way and conversion programme took place over three weekends and two weeks in early December 1995, when the final P.Way was installed at the old "E" junction to Canterbury and the

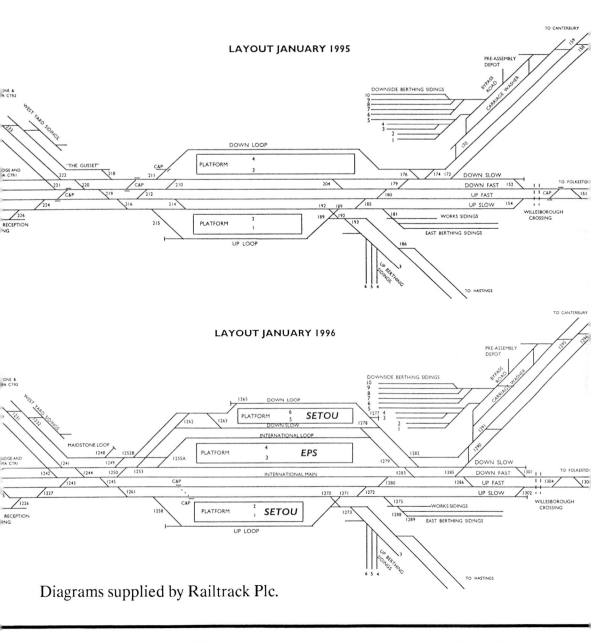

LAYOUT JANUARY 1995

LAYOUT JANUARY 1996

Diagrams supplied by Railtrack Plc.

changeover of all signalling in the Ashford area from the old Signal Box to the IECC. The IECC is now fully commissioned and has five Signalmans Workstations in operation to control the entire area from Elmstead Woods to Dover and the Channel Tunnel.

The signalling at Ashford is controlled by the IECC via three Solid State Interlockings (SSI's) and many of the tracks through, and approaching Ashford, are fully reversible, which greatly improves flexibility and will aid the Operators during future Engineering Works. In addition, between Ashford and the Channel Tunnel, the Up and Down lines have Full Bi-Directional Signalling, whilst between Ashford and Tonbridge, there is Simplified Bi-Directional Signalling in place.

In connection with the Resignalling, all the track circuits were changed to styles that provide immunisation against the three phase drive traction units that pass through Ashford. For the same reasons, the point machines were also changed to an immune style to prevent false operation, due to interference from the traction motors.

As an aid to the availability of the Signalling system, diverse cable routes were installed wherever possible, so that Data Links and Power cables are duplicated and fed from opposite directions. In respect of the Data Links, this diversity of routing can mean that links may go many miles along cable routes far remote from the equipment they control. Should one of the Signalling Power cables or SSI Data Links suffer damage or fail, the cables in the other route will still support the system. One part of the "ring main" is via Redhill and the other runs via Sevenoaks.

The IECC also incorporates Automatic Route Setting (ARS) throughout, which relieves the Signalmen of the requirement to set routes for most trains and movements in the area. The ARS is fully supported by access to the Master Timetables which helps it decide the priority and route that each train should follow. If necessary, the signalmen can override the system and set routes manually using his trackerball on the workstation.

In conjunction with the P.Way remodelling and resignalling, the Traction Supply was also strengthened to cater for the greater loads demanded by the increased traffic.

Ashford now has a fully modernised Railway Infrastructure and Station Buildings which are designed to handle some two million passengers per year and will take the station well into the 21st Century before the next renewal is required.

New signals at the London end of platforms 1 and 2 await commissioning as unit no. 930033 departs for Swanley on 11th October 1995 on a sandite application trip. Eurostar trains can apply their own sand but local electric stock inexplicably have never been so equipped. (V.Mitchell)

20. EUROSTAR
Jeremy de Souza
European Passenger Services

he dreams of engineers and industrialists finally became reality in late 1994, when the Channel Tunnel, a twin bore fixed rail link between Britain and France, opened to traffic. Built at a cost of almost £3bn, it links two of the most populated and industrialised nations on earth for the first time since the Ice Age.

Eurotunnel, an Anglo-French consortium, actually undertook the massive building project, and now operate the "Le Shuttle" service for vehicles between Folkestone and Calais. Railfreight Distribution (still part of British Rail in 1996) operates international freight trains through the tunnel. However, high speed passenger trains links are provided solely by Eurostar trains of European Passenger Services.

Each Eurostar train is a quarter of a mile long (approximately 400 metres) and carries up to 794 passengers. That's about the same as two fully loaded Boeing 747 Jumbo jets. Power cars at each end are electrically driven and provide up to 16500 hp to propel the eighteen passenger coaches in each formation efficiently and quietly.

The train's driver is certainly more akin to a pilot as he (or she) sits at the head of the sleek blue, grey and yellow train, surrounded by a complex array of computers, switches and dials. Two train managers circulate through the passenger areas, able to answer queries in at least two languages, and anything up to 12 catering staff offer drinks and snacks through the two buffet cars, or serve at-seat meals to the First Class passengers. All are attired in smart uniforms tailored by Pierre Balmain - one of Paris' most elegant fashion houses.

Already, Paris and London enjoy a regular service for most of the day, and with a gradual increase of traffic on the London to Brussels route, services continue to build on this axis too. About half of the trains to and from London stop at Ashford International. Never before have the three European capitals, and key regional towns along the route, had such convenient and stress-free connections. The London to Paris run takes just three hours, and Brussels only 15 minutes longer; from Ashford one can cut a good hour from these times. With such easy city centre to city centre connections, it is little wonder that more and more people are saying "I'll never fly again!"

But projects such as the Channel Tunnel, and Eurostar itself, don't come cheap, and many years, and billions of pounds, had to be invested in the planning and construction phases. The new trains, although related to the successful TGV units in France, were required to break new ground in their ability to cruise at high speed on the special lines, as well as draw power from three different power sources (the British 750volts DC, the French 25000 AC and the Belgian 3000 DC). On the specially built express lines in France, it was even realised that conventional signals would pass too fast for the drivers to see them, and so in-cab signals, safely achieved through advances in radio communication, were required. It is little wonder that each train cost £24m to build.

In Britain, while the complex wheels of local and central Government's planning processes grind inexorably forward to eventually permit the building of the UK's own high-speed line through Kent, yet more millions have been spent on upgrading the current routes out of London towards the Tunnel mouth near Folkestone to dovetail Eurostars trains into some of the busiest railway lines in the world.

The London railhead for the trains is itself a landmark for the 21st Century. The award winning Waterloo International Terminal can accommodate up to five Eurostar trains at any one time, and with its platforms, departure and arrival areas spread over different levels, has a working capacity of up to 6000 passengers per hour. The innovative blue steel and glass building, designed by British architect Nicholas Grimshaw, stand almost right beside the River Thames in the heart of London, adjoining Britain's largest domestic station.

Eurostar is operated jointly by state-owned organisations in each of the three countries it serves. SNCF and SNCB are the national railway companies of France and Belgium respectively, while in the UK, European Passenger Services Ltd, formerly a subsidiary of British Rail was created specially to manage operations in Britain.

From a limited start of operations in November 1994, the company was confident of capturing the lion's share of passenger traffic between London, Paris and Brussels, much of it from the airlines. In the first nine months of the service, over two million passengers took the train. Check-in times, which normally conjure up visions of crowded airport counters, have been cut to a mere 20 minutes, thanks to advanced ticket technology. Seat preferences and reservations can be made well in advance when actually booking the ticket, so that on arrival at Waterloo or Ashford, one has simply to pass a ticket validity check and security check before boarding. Naturally, the terminal boasts a selection of shops, bars and lounges for those who want to savour the experience.

However, even the operations described above are precursors to even more exciting developments. Early to mid 1996 will see the start of the second stage of Eurostar, and in addition, a whole new concept in night travel by train.

Eurostar was conceived and built with the primary notion of linking Paris, Brussels and London. But it soon became clear to its planners that it could also have a profound effect on other areas of the UK, which, through an extensive domestic rail network, be able to tap in readily to the opportunities of the Channel Tunnel.

Using the key trunk routes of the East and West Coast Main Lines, the

The 08.30 from Paris Nord speeds under the emegency evacuation bridges at the eastern ends of platforms 3 to 6 on 11th October 1995. Most of the 18 vehicles obscure the view of the former Ashford Works. (V.Mitchell)

Regional Eurostars will run direct to Paris and Brussels from Manchester and the West Midlands along the West Coast route, and from Glasgow and Edinburgh down through Newcastle and York along the East Coast route.

The trains will be slightly shorter than the classic Three Capitals units (fourteen coaches as opposed to eighteen), in order to fit into shorter domestic platforms. This said, they will still carry upward of 500 passengers per train, with all the comfortable benefits of Eurostar's service.

The trains will not call into Waterloo International, but will pass along the West London Line before accessing the rail routes to the Channel Tunnel near Clapham Junction.

The businessmen and women (and leisure travellers!) of most of the major industrial areas of Britain will have a viable alternative to air travel - smooth, fast and comfortable trains linking them right into the heart of the new Europe.

Planning ever bolder still, the third element of the international trains project will see yet another mould-breaking service commence in 1996.

Night trains, utilising a new generation of locomotives and purpose built sleeping cars and seated accommodation, are due to enter public service in the summer. Over £150m is currently being spent to develop the trains. Embracing the feeling of a "hotel on wheels", the trains will offer sleeper cabins equipped with en-suite toilets and even showers, as well as lounge cars for refreshments. For those travelling on a budget, each train will also convey carriages with reclining seats.

Early conceptual planning saw both Brussels and Paris served by trains from a number of regional British destinations. A review of passenger trends, however, has seen the market concentrated on Paris.

Every night, the trains will leave Plymouth, Swansea, Manchester and

Glasgow for the French capital. In addition, separate sleeping car trains, built to the same design, will leave London Waterloo International, for The Hague and Amsterdam, and for Cologne and a number of German destinations. These services are all expected to be very popular with business travellers keen to achieve a full day's work in another country, having fully rested while asleep during the night, as well as leisure travellers heading further afield.

Support from regional industrialists and public bodies throughout Britain is understandably high for both the day and night trains, as at long last they have their own tangible link, via the Tunnel, to the mainland of Europe.

Even with all these links finally in place, one can still see our own rail links as only one part of a much wider jigsaw. Connections from Lille, Paris and especially Brussels enable the imaginative passenger to reach right across Europe, and indeed, changing off Eurostar at Brussels Midi onto the "Ost-West Express" to Moscow, and then again at the Russian capital, one can catch the "Trans Siberian Express" all the way to Vladivostok!

Like air travel, it will almost be an operational necessity for effective and competitive communications. As flying made the world a smaller place, so the Channel Tunnel will convince the British that they are true Europeans, and that culturally and economically we will all benefit. If the first year of Eurostar's operation are anything to go by, we all have a very rosy future ahead indeed.

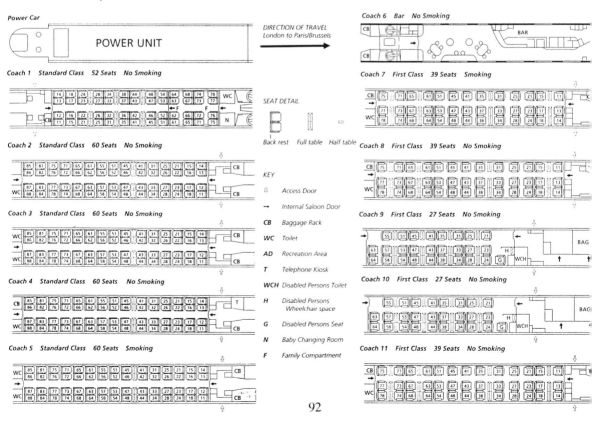

The 13.27 Waterloo to Brussels rushes past the remains of Ashford Works on 30th September 1995. The overgrown siding site on the right is planned to accommodate the Union Railway's tracks. (V.Mitchell)

Taken from the same footbridge as the previous picture, this shows the hand-worked Willesborough level crossing, much derided by the media who fail to realise that the construction of a junction with Union Railways nearby will result in its demise. Its temporary retention is thus forward looking. (V.Mitchell)

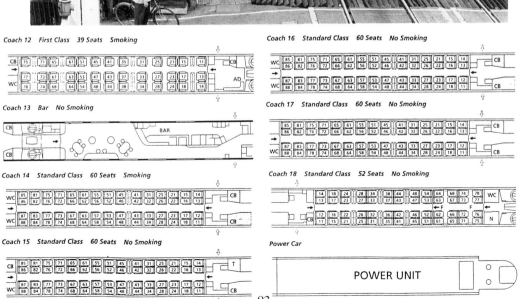

Coach 12   First Class   39 Seats   Smoking

Coach 13   Bar   No Smoking

Coach 14   Standard Class   60 Seats   Smoking

Coach 15   Standard Class   60 Seats   No Smoking

Coach 16   Standard Class   60 Seats   No Smoking

Coach 17   Standard Class   60 Seats   No Smoking

Coach 18   Standard Class   52 Seats   No Smoking

Power Car

POWER UNIT

21. EUROSTAR CONNECTIONS
Dave Ewart
South Eastern Trains

Continuing the town's long standing railway traditions, Ashford International remains a vital interchange for the South Eastern Train Company's services between London, Folkestone, Dover and the Thanet Coast and those of Network SouthCentral to Hastings, Eastbourne and Brighton.

The new South Eastern station, which has 400 car parking spaces for domestic service customers, is managed by a station manager who is also responsible for 80 staff and the management of ten stations between Paddock Wood and Folkestone.

No. 207202 **Brighton Royal Pavilion** passes the former Wagon Body Shop as it departs on 30th September 1995, working a fast service to Brighton. The extra coach in the centre provides the convenience of a lavatory. (V.Mitchell)

Frequent trains intensively used by business and leisure travellers link Ashford International with the popular resorts of Folkestone, Margate, Broadstairs and Ramsgate and London Victoria and Charing Cross, as well as the important commercial centres of Canterbury, Sevenoaks, Maidstone, Dover and Tonbridge. From May 1996, Ashford International will be served by some of the 16 new Networker Expresses which will dramatically improve service quality as they begin the replacement of older stock on Kent Coast routes.

In extending the Ashford to Hastings train service to provide direct links with Eastbourne, Lewes and Brighton for the first time in sixty years, South Eastern provided welcome new journey opportunities to customers throughout Kent and East Sussex.

Three Class 207 and one class 205 diesel electric multiple units which link Ashford International with Brighton have been lengthened from two to three coaches to improve seating capacity and quality of service for customers. To launch the new service in June 1995, two units were named *Ashford Fayre* and *Brighton Royal Pavilion* by respective civic dignitaries in a colourful costume ceremony at Ashford station.

The additional coaches are former class 411 electric multiple unit trailer coaches. They incorporate toilet facilities and are gangway connected to provide ready access throughout the train for refreshment trolleys.

Three daily direct limited-stop services in each direction link Ashford International, Hastings, Eastbourne, Lewes and Brighton in an overall journey time of around two hours. The Director of Passenger Rail Franchising has since directed that full responsibility for the route between Ashford, Hastings and Brighton, including all its services, will be taken by Network SouthCentral, and transfer from The South Eastern Train Company took place on 24th September 1995.

With the benefit of an attractive new Ashford International station, new trains and reduced journey times in prospect, the South Eastern Train Company looks forward to providing high quality services to an ever increasing number of customers.

Departures from 8 January 1996

	Mondays to Fridays			Saturdays			Sundays	
Brighton dep.	07.00	11.48	17.05	06.48	11.48	16.48	No through trains	
Ashford arr.	08.50	13.45	19.14	08.45	13.45	18.45		

	Mondays to Saturdays								Not Sat.
Ashford dep.	07.19	07.53	09.23	09.27	12.57	13.27	17.24	19.27	19.54
Paris arr.	10.23		12.23		16.05		20.29		22.53
Brussels arr.		11.10		12.44		16.44		22.45	

	Sundays						
Ashford dep.	09.23	09.57	12.57	13.27	17.24	19.27	20.24
Paris arr.	12.23		16.05		20.29		23.23
Brussels arr.		13.17		16.44		22.45	